"NO MATTER WHAT STEINBRENNER SAYS ABOUT ME, I'LL ALWAYS BE A YANKEE."

–Graig Nettles

BALLS

NETTLES SWINGS AWAY!

The manager kept getting fired and hired again, the star outfielder was arrested for beaning a seagull, the most famous member of the team never played an inning—he didn't have to, he was the owner. Welcome to the New York Yankees, and a profile in pandemonium by the man who never wanted to leave . . .

ON REGGIE JACKSON: "Reggie used the reporters. They thought they were smarter than he was, but all the time it was Reggie using them. He'd tell them a story exactly the way he wanted it, and he would get his headlines, and it made him in New York."

ON WINFIELD AND THE SEAGULL: "They took him right from the ballpark to the jail. He had to post a five-hundred-dollar bond before they let him out . . . We went to Detroit after the Toronto series, and when Winfield came to bat, all the fans in the center field bleachers stood up and started flapping their arms like seagulls."

Balls

Graig Nettles and Peter Golenbock

PUBLISHED BY POCKET BOOKS NEW YORK

POCKET BOOKS, a division of Simon & Schuster, Inc.
1230 Avenue of the Americas, New York, N.Y. 10020

Published by arrangement with G.P. Putnam's Sons
Library of Congress Catalog Card Number: 84-1866

ISBN: 0-671-54389-X

First Pocket Books printing April, 1985

10 9 8 7 6 5 4 3 2 1

POCKET and colophon are registered trademarks
of Simon & Schuster, Inc.

Printed in the U.S.A.

INTRODUCTION

Some kids dream of joining the circus, others of becoming a major league baseball player. I have been doubly blessed. As a member of the New York Yankees, I have gotten to do both. I have played third base for the Yankees since 1973, too many general managers, managers, and teammates ago to even count. A decade has seemed like a lifetime as a stream of new teammates continues to enter and leave the Yankee clubhouse with mad regularity.

On the Yankees, there have been but two constants: change and turmoil. The one thing I can say about playing with the Yankees is that it is rarely boring. Every day I cross the George Washington Bridge from my New Jersey home and I wonder, "What crazy thing is going to happen today?" They could make a soap opera out of our daily adventures and call it *As the Clubhouse Turns*.

At the end of last season, I was faced with a very difficult decision. My contract had run out. I became a free agent, and had I so chosen, I could have allowed my name to be placed into the free agent draft, where surely I would have been selected by several teams; perhaps by some willing to pay me more than what I ended up getting from the Yankees.

I decided not to do that. I love playing in New York with the Yankees. I love the New York fans, love the area, and I have to admit that though I am basically a private person at heart, I love the recognition playing with the Yankees brings me. I know it sounds contradictory, but that's the way it is. I have to admit I enjoy it when people come up to me and say, "Aren't you Graig Nettles of the New York Yankees?" One other thing I gradually came to admit to myself that I love about playing for the Yankees: being around the change and turmoil. When I signed again this fall, I knew it would be two more years of playing for what is probably the most bizarre sports franchise in America.

I began writing this book before the 1983 season began. When I started the book, I agreed to describe my baseball career, including my years in New York, as honestly and straightforwardly as I knew how. And now that I have re-signed with the Yankees, I am sticking to my agreement.

Since the advent of free agency and the coming of such owners as Ted Turner and George Steinbrenner, baseball has changed from a sport to a kind of show business with its hoopla, controversy, and razzamatazz. I suppose this book will add to the controversy that has been part of the team ever since I joined it back in 1973. If that happens, then I welcome it. After all, isn't controversy what playing for the Yankees is all about?

Someone once said that you have to have balls to play in New York and excel. He might have added, if you play for the Yankees, they better be big and brassy.

1

THE WINTER BEFORE
THE 1983 SEASON

I t is only a month after the end of the 1982 season, and I am still trying to recover from what has been a disastrous year, both for me and for the Yankees. The season was a fiasco. From the beginning we were unorganized. I had three managers, five pitching coaches, and dozens of teammates coming through a revolving door, some of whom were making a million dollars a year and sitting on the bench. It was such an unsettled situation that all the players were having problems because of it. We didn't have any direction. It was hard to concentrate on playing baseball.

Making things worse, George panicked when things didn't work out the way he expected at the beginning of the year. He had determined with the help of his crack baseball committee that the Yankees should be a speed team, not a power team. He ran Reggie Jackson out of town, said he didn't want Reggie on the Yankees anymore. And then when we didn't run, didn't steal bases, didn't play aggressively, he quickly dumped his original concept, and he began selling players, buying players, firing managers, firing ushers, making changes, screaming and yelling, yelling and screaming. Even if you had a scorecard, you couldn't keep everything straight.

In the middle of this disarray, I was playing poorly. I made a lot of errors I shouldn't have made, and they were costly ones. This is not an excuse, but in fairness it must be pointed out that I broke my thumb the first week of the season and never did recover from that. Later in the season I hurt my shoulder diving for a ball.

During a particularly bad streak, George started running me down in the newspapers, called me a has-been. He held a press conference to tell everyone he thought I was over the hill. He told reporters, "Nettles is in the twilight of his career, and if he never plays another game for me, he has earned more than what I have paid him." In effect, he was saying, "Thanks for the memories. See you later."

When he said that, it was picked up all across the country. Everywhere I went, all I heard was: "Graig Nettles is in the twilight of his career. He's over the hill. He's too old." And it depressed me, because the Yankee fans started booing me, and I've always had a great rapport with the fans. Also, it's much easier to play the game when you have the fans on your side.

Some players say that the booing doesn't get to them. They're lying. We would much rather have the fans adore us than hate us. And yet, when the fans started booing, I knew they were merely reflecting what they were reading in the papers. Since it's a two-team town, to keep my sanity I preferred to think that many of those who were booing me were Mets fans.

For the last two months of the season, I had difficulty

concentrating. In the field I continued making errors. In my mind, I kept thinking, "Am I old? Am I over the hill? Am I really through?" That's one thing George doesn't realize when he comes down hard on a player. It affects his play, whether for one game, or one week, or one month. It's very hard to play ball when you're catching hell from the front office, which in New York also means you're catching hell in the newspapers.

It stopped being fun coming to the ballpark. It's difficult to play well with stuff like that on your mind. It puts added pressure on you to produce, you start thinking that if you don't get a hit every time up, you're going to be benched forever. You go out there thinking, "Geeze, if I don't get a hit this time up," or "If I don't catch this ball," then I'm out of the lineup for a long time. You cannot play the game that way.

I started pressing in the field, and I lost my confidence, and as things were snowballing, I desperately needed a pat on the back from the manager. I needed him to say, "Hang in there. You're my man." But even though I continued to play, I didn't get it, because we didn't have a man like that. Our manager at the time was Gene Michael, and he was having too many of his own problems with George to help me. We had three managers in '82, and none of them could have had much confidence in themselves, knowing George was sitting behind them, ready to pull the plug. I was getting it from every side, and there was nobody to turn to. I couldn't help but feel that everyone was against me.

There is nothing worse than playing on a team when you know no one wants you. I knew I didn't fit into George's plans because of the things he had been saying about me, and so I told him to trade me away to the San Diego Padres if he could. I knew the Padres were looking for a third baseman, and San Diego is my hometown. I said to myself, "If that's the way he feels, I don't want to stick around where I'm not appreciated." Going to San Diego would have been ideal.

It didn't happen. Why, I don't really know. I never will know. George told me he gave the Padres a list of fifteen minor leaguers in the San Diego organization and said that if the Padres would give up any one of those players, George would trade me. But, George said, the Padres said no.

I can hardly believe that. The Padres wouldn't trade their number-fifteen minor leaguer for me? Maybe not the top prospect, but the fifteenth?

Now waiting for the 1983 season to begin my problems aren't only mental. My throwing arm is shot, and I don't know if it will ever come around. Late in the season against Kansas City I dove bare-handed to catch a foul pop, and when I hit the ground, I tore something in my shoulder. The shoulder is so sore that when I play catch with my kids, I can barely throw the ball thirty feet. The doctor prescribed rest and a regimen of exercises and stretching, and I am doing that, but the more I exercise, the more it hurts.

I am sure I can still hit major league pitching, but I also know that we are a team loaded with designated hitters.

BALLS

George just signed Don Baylor, who is one of the best
DHs around. We have Lou Piniella, Bobby Murcer, and
there's also Oscar Gamble. Hell, the only way I am going
to play is to be in there on defense. If I can't throw the
ball, I'm gone. As it is, George is looking for excuses to
get me out of there.

I don't want to end my major league career as a cripple.
When I go out, I want to go out still healthy. It's one more
complication. I just don't know what to do. They won't
trade me, and they won't play me, and I seriously doubt
they'll release me. Perhaps I'll be exiled to the Netherworld
of Kenny Holtzman. He was a pitcher George traded for because his thirteen-year-old son thought so highly of him. A
fine scout, George's son. When it turned out Kenny's arm
was no longer what it once was, George tried to trade him.
But Kenny, who had a no-trade clause in his contract, vetoed the trade and spent an entire season rotting on the
bench. His career was as good as over.

For most of the fall we had no idea who would be
managing in 1983. Clyde King was the third of George's
1982 managers, but few of us feel that Clyde was the
manager he really wanted. Clyde knows his baseball, but
he isn't very colorful. He doesn't put many fannies in the
seats, an important George criterion.

I don't think George has ever hired a manager he really
wants. I don't think he wants a manager at all. If he could
get away with it, he would be the manager. Except that if

he were manager, who would he blame if the team didn't win? I guess there's always the players.

I didn't know whether the new manager would be independent or another guy who would be merely George's puppet, a guy who would allow the owner to tell him who to play, a guy who would do what George wants, which is to bury me.

Now there is a glimmer of hope for me and for the Yankees. He has hired Billy Martin for a third time. Billy is the only manager we have ever had who stands up to George. He is the only manager who will fairly make up his mind about me and then decide whether I can still play or not. Billy's decision is going to be the one that will count. When my shoulder heals, I know I will be playing third base for the Yankees again. I will be able to continue playing this game.

After Billy held his press conference, the New York writers called me and said that Billy had praised me. Now I am happy to stay. I want to stay. Desperately.

Billy's hiring was a surprise to all the reporters, because most of them hate Billy and now are faced with the prospect of having to fight with him for yet another season. The reporters know too well what Billy thinks of them. He feels that it was the press who got him fired the first time, after his famous remark about Reggie Jackson and George: "One's a born liar, and the other's convicted." And Billy feels that wherever he goes, reporters lie in wait for him, trying to dig up dirt to hurt him. There's a certain amount of "everybody's against me" in Billy, and yet if you look at it objectively, you see that the reporters in New York are being paid to do exactly what he fears they are doing: dig up dirt to hurt him.

I'm sure some of the players are surprised that George hired Billy again. George and Billy are like Richard Burton and Liz Taylor. They are attracted to each other. They enjoy the glamour of having the other one around. Each respects the other for what he does for a team. Billy likes how George isn't afraid to spend money for players. George respects Billy's ability to walk into a chaotic situation, shake things up, and turn a team into a winner. It's something Billy's done wherever he's gone, and once Billy and Oakland split up, it seemed almost inevitable that George's magnet and Billy's love for the Yankees would pull Billy back to the Yankees again. The only question Billy's rehiring brings up is the same question that has come up every time Billy manages for George: Will George leave Billy alone so he can do his job? He never has in the past. I really don't see any reason why he should in the future. George is George. Billy is Billy. I wonder if George will do a 180 and make a trade to get Reggie back. Then it could be like the good old days again.

It's a week before spring training and I still can't throw a ball sixty feet, my shoulder hurts so badly. My wife, Ginger, has suggested I go see Dr. Chan, the acupuncturist who cured me when I was suffering from hepatitis in 1981. I don't understand how he did it back then, and I am skeptical he will be of any help this time, but in my desperate state, I have agreed to try anything, including a witch doctor. I hate needles, really hate them, and yet if I go to camp with a sore arm, a doctor well might say, "Have a shot of cortisone." Given a choice between the acupuncture needles and the cortisone needles, I have decided to opt for the acupuncturist.

I sit down in the chair, and Dr. Chan takes out the long, skinny, hairlike needles and sticks them into my shoulder. I wait for the pain, but there is none. He sticks a couple in my ear, hooks up electrodes to them, and turns on the juice. I go back to him four times, the final time just a few days before reporting to camp. For the first time since the summer, I can throw without pain.

If it hadn't been for him, I don't know what I would have done. I'm as surprised as anyone that I don't have any pain. I have a new arm and a manager who appreciates me. What more can a thirty-eight-year-old third baseman ask for?

With my contract running out at the end of this year, I told George that I would stay with the Yankees if he would give me a one-year extension through 1984. George said no. He said, "Let's see what happens this year, and then talk." He said that under no circumstances would he negotiate with me during the season. I figure he's betting that I'm going to spend most of the year on the bench, or that I won't do well, and at the end of the year he'll let me go.

George is convinced I am too old to be productive. It

appears that he doesn't want me anymore, that at the end of this season it is my turn for George's revolving door to spin me out into the street. The captain, it seems, is about to get his walking papers.

Part of it is my age. I'm thirty-eight. George is prejudiced against players over thirty-five.

When I was negotiating my last contract, during the '76 season, I was only thirty-two. George told a writer, "Do you think Graig is going to be my third baseman when he's thirty-seven? Come on." He had told me a year earlier that I wouldn't make it past age thirty-three. That's why he was very reluctant to give me a two- or three-year contract. He assumes that everyone in his mid-thirties is going to look like him at that age, and it's not the way it is. He doesn't realize that athletes have pride in their bodies. They're not going to just let themselves go like he did. It's hard to drill that through a person's mind who thinks one way. You try to win him over to your way of thinking, but it's hard to do. My problem right now is that he was so far out of shape by the time he was twenty-five that he can't imagine someone being in good shape at thirty-nine.

It's not hard to stay in good shape, really. The first thing you do is try not to eat four or five desserts a day like he does. He doesn't drink, so obviously he eats a lot to be as fat as he is. It's not so hard to take care of yourself when you realize that you can make a lot of money with your body. He doesn't realize that as an athlete, I know how to refuse a hot fudge sundae. He never could.

George may also be trying to phase me out because he has finally tired of my lip. Our worst confrontation occurred in the spring of 1977 after I had signed a contract which was worded in such a way that whatever deferred salary I was to get was going to be taxed. I didn't have an agent, and George had advised me to do it a certain way, and it turned out his advice was bad, and when I went to him to change the wording of the contract, he refused to do it.

I jumped the club in spring training to make him do something. I skipped a spring training game. George and Gabe Paul kept putting it off, putting it off, forcing me into a corner, and then when I acted, they made me look bad. I lost all respect for George and Gabe Paul because of that one.

By opening day, nothing had been resolved. Opening day I talked to George in Billy's office. This was ten minutes before taking the field for the first game of the season. I wanted that contract changed. I had a serious tax problem. And George wouldn't change it.

I lost control. I said, "Fuck you, you fat motherfucker." He said, "What?" I said, "You heard me. Fuck you, you fat motherfucker." I slammed the door in his face. That's why you need an agent. So things like that don't happen. I finally ended up taking the money as salary instead of deferring it. He didn't like that either. But I had to do it. He didn't give me any choice. And when my next contract came up, I decided to hire an agent.

After I slammed the door on him, I was figuring to myself, "Hell, I might be gone before the day is over," but instead I found out he liked it. George likes to be able to push people around, but if you stand up to him, he admires it. He tests people to see how far he can push them down, to see how much he can walk on them. If you don't let him, he looks up to you. He seems to try to antagonize people just to see how far he can push them. Maybe that's the way it is in business. Maybe that's what he does when he builds those big boats. I could live without that kind of testing.

Early in spring training I was interviewed on television. I was asked, "You've been captain for a year. Is it any different being captain?" I said, "Really, all I do as captain is take the lineups up to home plate before the game." The next question was, "How do you feel, and what are your feelings about playing this coming year?"

I said, "I feel fine. I'm healthy, and barring injury, I feel I can play 150 games."

The next day I got a call from my agent, Jerry Kapstein. He said that George had seen the interview and was all upset. George was screaming at Jerry, "What the hell is Nettles talking about wanting to play 150 games?" In the same breath George was hollering, "The captain is supposed to show some leadership out there. That's why he's captain. To show leadership."

On one hand he was telling my agent he didn't see me playing regularly. On the other hand he was questioning my role as leader, which has no relationship to my being captain. You lead by example, not by title. My first question to Jerry was, "How am I going to show leadership if I'm not playing?" Here's a Catch-22 if I ever heard one. How can I? You can't be the leader of a ballclub sitting on the bench. And you know, by saying I wanted to play in 150 games, I thought I was saying the right thing at the time. I thought I was saying something he would have wanted to hear. I know if I was the owner, I'd want every player on my club to say he wants to play at least 150 games.

I went and talked to Billy about it, and Billy said, "Graig, don't worry about it. You'll play as much as I want you to, depending on how well you're playing." So that was all I needed. And it seems that I am finally in a good situation. I don't have to worry about managers playing guys George wants to play. Billy's the manager, and he's on my side. In the past other managers have said, *"We've* decided to do this." And when they say "we," they mean George and I have decided. Billy says "I," not "we." Billy knows what I have done for him in the past, and he knows what I can do for him.

The atmosphere has been much better this year than last. Some of the guys didn't know what to expect from Billy. They had never played for him, and they had heard stories and were a little fearful. Some of the players who had played against him were wondering what he would be like, because if you play against him, you hate him.

I was telling Steve Kemp and Don Baylor and Roy Smalley that there was no reason to fear him, that it's really very easy to play for Billy if you work hard and don't give him any excuses.

And when Billy arrived, we went out and worked on fundamentals more than we ever had done before—pitchers covering first base on hits to the right side, bunting plays, run-down plays, double steals, all the things we hadn't done much in the past couple years—Billy made us do these things over and over and over again. Billy believes in repetition, and that's why he's always been so successful.

Billy runs camp like it's the army. He's the general, and he has his officers doing things for him. Lee Walls was with him in Oakland and knows how he wants things done, and Art Fowler, his pitching coach, has been with him for years. And it's very organized. Every coach knows what to do, so the players learn to do things Billy's way.

It has been a very positive camp. There is no standing around, which is what you find in many camps. The pitchers get their throwing in, run, and get the hell out of there, where in most camps pitchers shag flies, and there's a lot of boredom. I'd say that with Billy's camp this year there was the least amount of boredom in many a year.

The players are split into two fields, and either you're hitting in a cage against live pitching or you're fielding ground balls. You're always involved, you are never standing around in the outfield for hours on end, waiting for that one fly ball to come along. Why should you ever have a pitcher standing in the outfield? Only outfielders should be out there, working on getting a jump off the bat rather than having to worry about running over a bunch of pitchers standing out there killing time.

Everyone has the feeling that Billy's going to take this team and turn it into a winner. It's such a change from last year.

When I arrived at Fort Lauderdale, Billy was very good to me. He asked, "Do you want to play a little or a lot?'' I said, ''I want to play a little bit in the beginning and then in the last two weeks I'd like to start playing every day to get myself in shape.'' He said, ''Fine.''

I was able to miss a lot of the early games, which was fine with me, because once I'm feeling good and get my stroke down, I'm ready to start the season, and I want to play every day. It only takes seven or eight spring training games for me to be ready. If you get in the groove too early, you just seem to fall into bad habits. I feel good physically, and I've been hitting and fielding well, and I'm ready.

George has been uncharacteristically quiet during spring training. He had been so brutal toward us the first half of last year that in August the players requested a meeting with him. We said, ''George, we don't like to open the papers every day and see you blasting our ass. It doesn't set well with us, and it doesn't make us better players. Please stop.'' He listened and was sympathetic. He said he would take it easy on us in the future, and so far he has. His silence may also be part of a deal that he and Billy worked out. In the past Billy often complained about George's second-guessing and about his blasting everyone in the papers. Maybe as part of the deal to come back to the Yankees, Billy got George to keep quiet. Or maybe we're seeing a new George. If this keeps up, the newspaper reporters are going to have to figure out a way to stir up trouble. They don't like it when it's quiet. It doesn't sell newspapers. George doesn't like it either. It doesn't sell tickets.

Toward the end of spring training, Billy gave us a talk. He said, "Let's start opening day and kick their butts. Let's go out and get off on a winning streak. Then let the other teams try to catch us." That's what Billy did when he took over the A's in 1981. They won something like twenty out of twenty-one, and they were way ahead in June, when the players went on strike, and they made the playoffs. The Yankees have never been that kind of team, though. We rarely get off to a good start and run away with it, because every year we have three or four or ten new teammates, and it always takes us a couple of months to get used to playing together.

The only time we started fast in all the years I've played with the Yankees was in 1976. Billy had taken over in the middle of the 1975 season, and he and Gabe Paul made the moves they thought they had to make to win a pennant, and the next year we got off to a fast start and won the pennant wire to wire. It was also the year George didn't interfere much except toward the end when we lost a few games in a row and our lead was cut from ten to seven games. For a few days there, he started to panic, and he was screaming and threatening to fire Billy, but we began winning again and he quieted down.

Last year George was in a state of panic all year long. We didn't win the first week, and it was panic time. Boom, there was a big turnover in personnel, and throughout the whole year, there was nothing but panic, with no one in the organization with a strong enough personality to stop him.

This is what makes Billy's being here so important. I think—at least I hope—that Billy would not allow that to happen. Billy has told me he is going to run the club, not George. He knows he has full authority, that we will live and die under Billy's authority. And most of the guys are happy about that. Not that everybody is going to be happy playing under Billy. He knows you can't please twenty-five guys. Billy always said that his philosophy was to keep the five guys who hated him away from the five who weren't sure.

2

1944—1969

I'm the only Graig I've ever known. I've run across a few people who have named their kids after me, because they liked the name, not because I was close to them. Matt Keough's brother, Joe, who used to play in the big leagues, named his kid Graig, using my spelling. He liked the way Graig sounded. My mom didn't like Craig and she didn't like Greg, so she combined the two of them. My Dad was away at the war, so he didn't have any say.

I never knew I had a strange name until I got to high school, when everyone kept misspelling and mispronouncing it. To this day one of my pet peeves is people who think they know me real well but who call me Craig. If they know me that well, they should take the time to know how to spell my name.

My father was an Okie. He came out to San Diego in the early thirties during the Depression and the Dust Bowl. Dad, whose name is Wayne, and his twin brother, Bill, hopped freight trains across. In Claremore, which is twenty-five miles from Tulsa in northwestern Oklahoma, there was no work for them, so their mom gave them her blessing and said go on, I hope everything works out. Dad told me he and Bill got separated somewhere in Oklahoma, ended up on different trains and were separated for weeks, but after hopping from train to train, they ended up coming into San Diego on the same train.

They were determined to make something of themselves, and they became football stars at San Diego State, and then they both joined the police force in San Diego, and my dad did that for ten years, and quit to teach high school. He retired a few years back.

He met my mom at San Diego State. She was from the mining town of Bisbee, Arizona. I don't know how she got to San Diego. And I'm not sure how they met. But they did, and they married in 1941, and I was born in 1944.

My dad started me playing ball when I was four or five. He encouraged me to play at the playgrounds, and I was always outdoors, playing ball. From him I learned the joy of playing baseball. Especially when there's sunshine every day.

San Diego High School was in a very mixed part of town. A lot of guys ended up going the wrong way, but it was a great athletic school. It turned out some big league ballplayers before me. Floyd Robinson, Deron Johnson. We had kids from the richest part of the city and from the poorest. It was a melting pot. It prepared you for life. There were fights, there were gangs. I stayed out of that because I was playing sports all the time. There were some bad actors in the school: Anglos, Mexicans, Portuguese, Italians, blacks. You learned to live with different types of people. You learned to get along. I was the only white guy on our basketball team. Fourteen blacks and me.

In high school I was a second baseman and shortstop. I wasn't that great. Wasn't all-league. Hit about .260. I was small. As a sophomore I weighed ninety-five pounds. I didn't get bigger until I got into college. In high school I was a much better basketball player and earned a scholarship. In college, I started putting on weight, which slowed me down in basketball, but helped me immensely in baseball. Made me a power hitter.

While still in college, at San Diego State, I played top semi-pro ball in Alaska for two years. My team got us jobs in Fairbanks, where we played, and the pay was good. We played ball every night. Most of the players were from USC, Arizona State, and other colleges in California. On my team were Rick Monday, Tom Seaver, Andy Messersmith, Gary Sutherland, and a pitcher named Mike Paul. We played sixty games and won fifty of them. We played some army teams. One game Seaver struck out twenty batters. He overpowered them. One year playing against ex–big league ballplayers our Fairbanks team finished second in a national tournament in Wichita, Kansas.

The first night in Fairbanks, I was getting the grand tour of the town, and we walked into a bar about ten at night, and we walked out of there at one-thirty, and the sun was shining right in my face. I said, "How long have we been in here?" My guide said, "The sun sets at eleven-thirty and comes up at twelve-thirty." We had twenty-three hours of daylight. We put tinfoil all over the windows so we could sleep.

Monday and I had a few jobs, but we kept quitting or got fired. They had us loading trucks for ten hours a day. Then they wanted us to play ball at night. We couldn't do it. We told them, "We're here to play ball. Find us an easier job." Then we worked construction, but all we did was clean up the construction site. Later Rick went and sold used cars. The jobs got softer for us, because they realized we couldn't do manual jobs and then play ball at night.

In '64 there was a question whether Monday or I was going to be kept on the team to go to the tournament in Wichita. Both of us were outfielders, and there was only room for one of us, and he was hitting .230, and I was hitting .260, so they decided to keep me and send him home. And he was the number-one pick of the first year of the free agent draft in '65. He got $104,000, and I got $15,000.

After my junior year in 1965, I was undecided whether to sign a pro contract in baseball with the Minnesota Twins or go back to college for my senior year. That year, '65, the Twins won the American League pennant, and for all I knew they were a great organization.

I was a fourth-round pick, and I didn't get much of a bonus. The Twins offered me fifteen thousand dollars. I was holding out for twenty thousand dollars, and finally, after the summer was over, I decided, "What's five thousand dollars over the long run? I want to find out if I can play professional baseball." I swallowed my pride and took the lesser money. It wouldn't be the first time I ended up with lesser money.

My first spring training was in Melbourne, Florida. I didn't know how good the other players were. I watched the rookies, and I saw players who had been around two, three years, and some of them looked like they couldn't have made my high school team. I didn't know that the caliber of ball was so good in California that the players from other parts of the country wouldn't be that great. I was shocked that there were players who had signed professional contracts who couldn't have made my high school team. That gave me a lot of confidence.

Before I came to camp, I vowed I'd give it three years to see if I was going to be any good at it or not, but right away I knew that I'd get to the high minor leagues pretty quickly.

I thought I should have started out at Double-A, and at Wisconsin Rapids, which was Single-A, the competition was less than it should have been. I was twenty-one, and a lot of the other kids were seventeen and eighteen. That's why it didn't surprise me to lead the league with twenty-eight home runs.

From there I went to Double-A in Charlotte, North Carolina, and I led that league in home runs with nineteen. All I remember are big ballparks and long road trips. When the Charlotte season ended I got called up to the Twins the last month of that season, '67. I wasn't ready for the big leagues, but it was a chance for me to get the feel of what it's like to play with the big boys. Billy was there as a coach. I was there a month and got into three games, hitting one for three. That was the year the pennant race came down to four teams in the final weekend of the season. We went to Boston the last two games, and we had to win just one out of the two, and Boston beat us both games. Yaz went seven for eight and won the Triple Crown. I sat on the bench and watched.

The Red Sox had their star Jim Lonborg rested, but decided not to pitch him the first game and pitched Jose Santiago instead. We pitched Jim Kaat, and he was blowing them away for five innings, they couldn't touch him, when all of a sudden something popped in his elbow, and he had to come out of the game. The reliever got hit hard, and they beat us.

They saved Lonborg for the final game. We couldn't understand why the Red Sox didn't go with their best pitcher in the first game. So it was Lonborg against Dean Chance, who had won twenty games for us that year. Those were the days when the pitchers used to warm up at Fenway Park right by the dugout. I went and grabbed a bat and stood nearby while Dean was warming up. He was throwing a fastball that was moving a foot, and his slider wasn't breaking very sharply, and I was thinking, "They won't hit him. He's unhittable."

We got out there, and the Red Sox pounded the hell out of Dean Chance. He was gone about the third inning, and I'm sitting on the bench, thinking to myself, "I don't know if I'm going to be able to play in this league if those guys can hit a guy who's throwing that good." I later found out that a lot of pitchers leave their good stuff right there on the sidelines. When they get into the game, the ball seems to straighten out a lot. At the time I didn't understand that part of the game. The Red Sox beat us, and we lost the pennant.

That year Minnesota had a veteran ballclub, and I

learned a lot from those guys. They were down that we had lost, but there was no crying, no temper tantrums. They accepted it and were very gentlemanly about it.

I could see how those guys never got too up for a game or too down. And I adopted that philosophy. I just take things as they come. If you win, that's great, and if you lose, there's no way breaking a seat on an airplane or punching a wall or breaking a light bulb can change that result.

In 1968 I was promoted to Triple-A ball and I played for Denver. Billy Martin was my manager. The first month or so I didn't like him. To be more precise, I hated him. He didn't think much of me on the field, and he would take me out for defense. He jumped all over me. He would yell and scream at me. He yelled and screamed whenever a player made a mistake. He'd scream right in the dugout in front of the other players after you came in from the field. "Goddammit, why didn't you take the extra base? Jesus Christ, can't you tell the guy in right field has a weak arm? What the hell is wrong with your brain? Are you a dummy?" I never had a manager do that.

The first couple of weeks our manager had been John Goryl, a mild-mannered guy. We were in last place. Then Billy took over. Billy didn't think much of college guys. He held us in contempt, the same way he holds National League players in contempt. He felt we thought too much, that we hadn't scuffled around enough in life, that we had it too easy all our lives, that we weren't hungry enough. And so what he did, he put us through hell, the same way the army puts you through boot camp to toughen you up, and after about a month I began to understand that the reason Billy did all that screaming and yelling was so you wouldn't make the same mistake again. He forced you to think while you were out on the field, made you aware of what was going on on the other club, who could throw, who could run, the right thing to do in every situation. Ordinarily they don't teach you this in the minors. Billy wanted us to always be thinking. He drilled it into my head, "Figure out how fast the batter is so you'll know what to do when the ball is hit to you. If he's slow, you have plenty of time. If he's fast, you can't waste time. If there's a runner on second and a ball is hit to left, if the runner is fast, cut the throw. If he's slow, let it go through." These are the little things he taught me that I use to this day.

One time he took me out of a game in my hometown of San Diego, which embarrassed the hell out of me. He waited until I was on the field, then he called time, and then he sent someone else out there to replace me. He was letting me know that he was going to be the boss of the ballclub, that the players were not going to run the team, that he was. And I have since learned that for a ballclub to win, the manager has to have the respect of the players, and the manager has to be boss. The manager has got to be the leader, not the players, and this was the message Billy was giving us. Things had to be done his way.

And when we did them his way, we started to win. We played Billy Martin baseball. We stole bases, used the squeeze play, bunted men around, and played exciting, heads-up baseball, the hard-nosed way he plays the game. He took that team, which was in last place, and he made us into pennant winners. When I saw the results, I stopped hating Billy Martin, and I began to see him for what he was: an extraordinary leader. Billy has always said that if you follow him, he will lead you to victory. The problem Billy has is that it isn't always easy for a major league player to make that leap of faith. Some players will not respect the manager, no matter who he is. Reggie is one of those players.

And the next year, when Billy began managing in the majors at Minnesota, he wasn't any different, except that he didn't yell at the veterans. The veterans knew him and respected him, and he turned them around and taught them how to win. And it isn't any different today. On a Billy Martin team, there is only one boss: Billy Martin. And if you do it his way, you'll win.

In '69 Billy was promoted to manager of the Twins, and he took me with him. I was the opening-day left fielder, and I platooned with Cesar Tovar in left field because Harmon Killebrew was the third baseman. He hit forty-five home runs that year. I played about fifteen games at third base and did well. But Billy got fired, and I was traded to Cleveland. I don't really know why Twins owner Calvin Griffith fired Billy, but I'm sure that Calvin would call Billy up to the office to talk about the games, and Billy wouldn't go. He didn't want to listen to ole Calvin. I didn't think they were having serious problems, because we were winning. But then halfway through the winter, Billy got fired, and I was traded. I had made one error in the outfield and one at third base. When I got to Cleveland, the first thing I read about myself was, "He's a good hitter but he can't play third base."

BALLS

I was in Venezuela playing winter ball when I heard about the trade. I got a call from Alvin Dark, who was managing the Indians then. He said, "I'm Alvin Dark, and I hear you can play third base." I said, "Yes, I can." He said, "Good. When you get to spring training, you're my third baseman." I said, "Thanks, Alvin, that's all I ever wanted."

3

APRIL 1983

The 1983 season is off and running, and we started the way we usually do—win one, lose one. Our pitching has been inconsistent. I question whether our staff is going to be deep enough to win this year. Ron Guidry is good for twenty every year. You never have to worry about him.

Shane Rawley is pitching very well. It was Jeff Torborg's idea to make him a starter last year. As a reliever, you have to come in and throw fastballs or sliders to overpower the hitters, but as a starter Shane can use his changeup much more effectively, and he has been just super for us.

Shane's a quiet guy. He's single, and I very rarely see him off the field. When things don't go well, he has a tendency to get down on himself. If someone gets a cheap hit off him, he'll get down, and then he loses concentration and starts giving up more hits. Instead of going harder after the next hitter, he gets in even more trouble.

I've been tempted to go out to the mound and talk to him, but it should be the catcher's job to shake him up, not mine. Cheap hits are part of the game, and you can't let them bother you if you're going to be successful.

Every year there seems to be one pitcher on the staff who has bad luck, and last year it was Shane. Everything they hit dribbled through the infield or just barely fell over the infielder's head. I don't know why it happens, but it sure happened to him. I expect that this year his luck will change.

Dave Righetti had a lousy season last year because he had five different pitching coaches. Here's a kid with the kind of arm that comes along once every ten years and a good head, and here were four or five guys telling him their theories of pitching, and he was listening to all of them, trying everything they said, and he became so screwed-up he found himself back in the minors. Every pitching coach has his theory of how you should hold the ball, wind up, dip your shoulder, follow through, and it would have been a miracle if he hadn't screwed himself up. This year there will be one manager, and one pitching coach, Art Fowler, and the records of Rags and Guidry, most of all, will reflect that.

Bob Shirley is a bulldog. He's a competitor, has a lot of heart, and won't back down on any hitter. He looked very impressive during spring training, and then he went out and got hit hard his first game in Seattle, and boom, right away he was out of the rotation because of something he said to Art Fowler.

Bob Shirley is another one of the silent guys on our team. He doesn't say much in the clubhouse, and on the field he doesn't say a whole lot either. But when he's on the mound, he's a different person.

Shirley got upset because Art called time and came out to the mound and told him to throw a certain pitch to a certain hitter. That hitter then hit Art's suggestion out of the ballpark to beat him. After the game, Bob told Art, "Don't ever come out and tell me what pitch to throw." That's the kind of guy Shirley is. He's got a lot of guts. He wants to pitch his own game, and he feels he's been around and knows what pitches to throw. And when you butt heads with Art, you basically are butting heads with Billy, and Billy took him out of the rotation. The trouble is, with Shirley out of there, we really don't have anyone else as fourth starter. Jay Howell looked overpowering in spring training, but since the regular season began, he's been having trouble getting hitters out. He keeps developing a blister on his middle finger, and it gets bad after five innings. Also, after Guidry, Righetti, and Rawley, the hitters see Howell, and they say to themselves, "Finally, a rookie," and it gives them confidence. Jay needs a year or two under his belt so they will fear him a little more.

It isn't entirely the pitchers' fault that we played five hundred ball in April. The hitting hasn't been consistent either.

We began the season with three games in Seattle, and lost the first two. For some reason we've never done very well in the Kingdome. Our record since it opened is something like ten and thirty-two. Why, I don't know. They're a last-place team year after year, but they seem to get fired up playing the Yankees. They get their biggest crowds when we come to town. It's supposed to be a nice park to hit in, but the lighting isn't very good, and I don't see the ball that well. The Mariners just seem to get ahead of us early. And when they don't do that, they beat us late.

We faced Gaylord Perry in the opener. He's a very good competitor. You know the situations when he's going to throw you a spitter, and you know it's coming, but it's still a very hard pitch to hit. He played with us for a few months, and we all know how he does it, and he's still hard to detect. He puts Vaseline all over his body, and before he goes into his windup, he touches behind his neck, goes to his belt, goes to his hat, goes to his neck again, and he keeps repeating, and a lot of times he picks up the rosin bag and loads his hand with rosin, and as he releases the ball, it comes out of what seems like a big puff of smoke.

Gaylord has so many tricks, and you know you're going to have to battle him hard. You know you're not going to get anything good to hit, that every pitch he has something up his sleeve. Literally.

The next day we got beat by a kid named Young, a rookie left-hander who was very impressive. The kid is only a couple years out of college. He had poise and control, and he looks like he knows how to pitch. You see kids like him all the time: they've made it to the big leagues, and they're pumped up and they're playing the

Yankees, and they pitch like crazy. And then the travel-ing starts, and sooner or later the bubble bursts and they come down to earth. But that night he pitched a very good ballgame and beat us.

Righetti finally got us our first win.

After Seattle, we flew to Toronto, where we had an in-ning that conceivably could have cost us a pennant before we even got started.

We were ahead by a run late in the game, and the Jays had the bases loaded with two outs. Goose was pitching in relief of Doyle Alexander, who for the second game in a row had pitched beautifully. The Blue Jay catcher—I don't know the guy's name; I don't know the names of many of the Toronto players except the ones who used to play with us—hit a pop fly into right center field. It was a cold day, and windy, and Willie Randolph was running back for the ball, and Jerry Mumphrey and Steve Kemp were rushing in from the outfield. Mumphrey was calling for it, but Willie couldn't hear him over the wind, and Kemp couldn't hear because before the game he stuffed cotton in his ears because the wind was bothering him. Before the game Kemp was complaining, "It's blowing right through my ears," and though I had never seen any-one do this before, he went and stuffed balls of cotton in his ears. As the ball dropped into the palm of Willie's glove, Kemp slammed into Willie and stepped on Mum-phrey's toe. The ball fell loose, the tying run scored, and both Jerry and Steve were injured. The next guy up then hit one of Goose's fastballs into the seats for three runs and the ballgame.

After the game, doctors said Mumphrey had a broken

toe and Kemp a severely banged-up shoulder. We're
going to need both those guys if we're going to win. I've
always admired Kemp. No one hustles like he does. No
one has ever had to say to him, "Get the lead out." But
you can be sure that now it'll be, "Hey Steve, get the cotton out."

The biggest problem right now is that the Yankees
have too many good players. It always seems to be that
way, and every year it hurts us badly. It's not enough
for George to have one good team. He always has a
team and a half or two good teams, which is to your ad-
vantage if someone important gets hurt. But unless
that happens, you've got a lot of unhappy good players
sitting around, especially when George has promised
each of five high-priced athletes that he is going to be a
starting outfielder.

I feel for Oscar Gamble. Like me, Oscar is also in the
last year of his contract, and he says George promised
him a multi-year contract in Florida, but now that the season has started George keeps canceling appointments
with his agent. Oscar called George a liar in the papers
and told reporters he wants to be traded.

Oscar says he should be playing. He says he could hit
thirty home runs a year playing in Yankee Stadium if they
would only let him play. Oscar proved how solid a player
he was in 1976 when he was our right fielder our first

pennant year. The next year he was traded to the White Sox for Bucky Dent and he hit thirty home runs. Oscar says he feels fine. George says he has a sore shoulder. He isn't playing, and he's not being given the chance to show anything. If he doesn't get to play it has to cost him money on the free agent market.

I'm luckier than Oscar in that Billy has told me I'm going to be playing every day. Either I do well, or I fall flat on my face, but at least I get a chance to prove my worth. Oscar, on the other hand, will only get to show his worth in batting practice, and there aren't too many scouts who go by what you do in batting practice.

My one question about Oscar is whether George is punishing him for vetoing a trade last year for Al Oliver. After Oscar vetoed the trade, Oliver was traded to Montreal where he led the team in hitting and RBIs. George had figured Oliver was the guy we needed, but he traded Oscar for him without checking into Oscar's contract, and then when Oscar said no, it turned out there were only certain teams Oscar would okay a trade to, and Texas was not one of them. Oscar had already been to Texas, and he really disliked it there. So instead of the Yankees quietly saying, "Okay, Oscar, you have every right not to go," which they should have done, they made it sound like the deal was all set and that at the last minute Oscar nixed it, which was not the way it happened at all.

And it's ironic. The way Oscar came back to us in the first place was through a screw-up in the Yankee front office. We had made a trade with Texas and announced the two minor league players in the deal before they cleared waivers, so the commissioner stepped in and awarded Oscar to the Yankees. Now he's probably sorry he came back.

Mumphrey is unhappy too. Billy is keeping him on the bench against right-handers and playing Ken Griffey in center. Everybody feels for Mumphrey. He isn't causing trouble, because he hardly says a word to anybody, but it is out of character to hear him grumbling in the press. Maybe he feels he has to do this to get traded someplace where he can play every day. He wouldn't be the first.

Jerry has been getting murdered in the papers. The writers are saying that Jerry isn't a winning ballplayer, that he doesn't drive in enough runs, that he's only a mediocre fielder, that Billy doesn't like him. You read this sort of stuff, but you try hard not to pay attention. The New York writers are paid to try to start feuds. Nevertheless, you read enough of that stuff, and it begins to affect your play.

Billy doesn't like his players popping off in the press about him, and this is not going to endear Mumph to Billy. But Billy also knows that Mumphrey is not a clubhouse lawyer, that he's no troublemaker. A guy like that starts talking about a manager behind his back, and before you know it, there's a mutiny. But that isn't Jerry's way. He rarely talks to anyone else. He just goes quietly about his business.

Catching is a touchy situation. Both Rick Cerone and Butch Wynegar want to play every day, and they can't, and Billy seems to be using Wynegar more often. Rick is pretty depressed right now. He's not doing well, and then when Wynegar plays, Wynegar does do well. It's possible Rick would okay a trade, but he wants to play here. Right now Wynegar is doing the better job, and Billy has to stick with the better catcher.

I knew the odd-day catching system wasn't going to work for very long. I don't know who they thought they were kidding with that. It's like what they tried to do with Sparky Lyle and Goose. Sparky was supposed to pitch to the lefties and Goose to the righties. But that's not the way it works with relief pitchers. If a relief pitcher is good, he doesn't care whether the batter is lefty or righty. The theories these people come up with are just stupid. "Sparky can come in and get the left-handers out, and we can call on Goose to get the right-handers out . . ." It just doesn't work that way. A relief pitcher has to know in his own mind that he is the number-one honcho out there and that he can get anyone who walks up to the plate out. That's the way the good relievers think. They should have learned their lesson in the way the Sparky and Goose thing was handled, that it was not going to work catching Cerone and Wynegar every other day.

You can platoon a third baseman, or a first baseman, or a left fielder, but to platoon a catcher or relief pitcher, that just doesn't work.

Every once in a while I see Rick when he's in a funky mood, when he wants to say something to the press, and I'll quietly tell him to zip it, to try to hold it in. Because you don't win by going to the press. In fact, at a meeting George said, "Don't challenge me in the press because you can't win." And he's right. You can't. If you have a gripe, you go to the manager or the owner. Don't go to the press. Though it's a temptation, because when the reporters start asking you questions about why you're not playing, you badly want to say something. You have to think about it a few seconds and shut up.

So far, the players have been good about that, because they have confidence that Billy is going to run the show. He'll do it his way, and in the long run it'll be the right way.

Even Don Baylor has been up to see Billy. Billy kept Don on the bench against Dave Stieb, a tough right-hander, and used Bobby Murcer to DH. After the game Baylor went right in to see Billy. "I don't like sitting—ever," Baylor told him.

We also have problems at shortstop. George wants Billy to play Andre Robertson there, and Billy wants to play Roy Smalley. I'd prefer Bucky Dent back.

We had a very fine team with Bucky as shortstop, and there was no reason at all to trade Bucky away and to trade Ron Davis to Minnesota for Smalley. Bucky was playing an excellent shortstop. So he hit .230. He caught every ball hit his way, and to this day I don't know why in the world they insisted on having a shortstop who hit thirty points higher, when what we needed most was excellent defense. I know this: Bucky was as good a shortstop as I've ever played with. We had a great rapport. It was as though we could sense where the other was going to be. Sometimes the ball would go toward the hole, and in an instant I knew I could get it if I dived, but I would know that Bucky was going to be there, so I didn't have to dive for it. I never have that feeling with Smalley. Plus the fact that Roy doesn't have much range going up the middle, so he plays so far to his left that I have to cover just about the entire left side of the infield. Last year they wrote that I had lost my range. Well, hell, it wasn't that. It was that I was playing with a different shortstop. We have a lot of left-handed pitching, and I have to play a little closer to the line, and yet the shortstop is playing way up the middle, so there's a huge hole I have to cover all by myself. There were times when I had to dive to my left for a ball, and afterward I went and looked, and my skid marks are closer to second base than they are to third. It's very disheartening for a third baseman to know he has to cover so much ground.

The ones who should be bitching are the pitchers. They're getting hurt the most. Against the White Sox Righetti lost a no-hitter on a ball I thought was hit directly at shortstop. Roy was playing up the middle and a kid named Kuntz hit a ball directly at shortstop, and I was astounded that he wasn't anywhere near it. It was ruled a base hit, and Righetti ended up giving up two hits that night.

Billy knows this. I told him. I begged him, "Please get Smalley to play more straightaway." Billy said he'd keep an eye on it and see what he could do about it.

Billy's starting to ease Andre Robertson into the lineup, which makes things much easier for me. When Andre's in there, I know that a ball to my left is probably going to be caught.

Billy has been trying a lineup with Andre at shortstop and Smalley at first, but that's a different problem, because what do you do with Griffey, who is one of our better hitters? Just because we have so many guys who deserve to play, Billy is going to constantly have to be juggling and shuffling until there is a major injury.

When I came into the clubhouse before one of the home games, I was introduced to a big kid who turned out to be the Stanford quarterback, John Elway, who George wants to sign as an outfielder.

I don't care one way or the other—most of the guys don't, but I just think that life could be miserable for the kid in the minors, even if he's making the million dollars a year George is dangling at him. Yes, he'd have his money, but he'd be stuck all summer with a bunch of guys struggling along at $500 a month, and there would be an awful lot of jealousy. And the fans in those minor league towns could really make it tough, because he better hit .400 and field like Joe DiMaggio, or he's going to hear about it. And I've heard he's not a "can't miss" player. He's just a good player, not the type of player you would ordinarily give that kind of money to, but this is one of those cases where George is trying to milk the kid for all the publicity he can get. Baseball is show business to George, and if he could lure the kid away from football, George figures the kid would bring people into the ballpark. And you know, from a business standpoint it's not a bad idea. The only problem is that you can never really know how good a young kid like this is.

Certainly, if George invests a ton of money in him, he's going to make sure the kid makes it to the big leagues, whether he can play or not.

And yet I read that there's a clause in his contract that

if he isn't happy with baseball after two years he can go back to football. How can George do something like that? Hand a guy a million a year to play at Fort Lauderdale and another million to play at Nashville and then find out the kid doesn't like it?

We got guys on the big club fighting for contracts, guys like myself, Oscar Gamble, Goose, and a few others, and they wonder why George is throwing all this money to a kid who hasn't proved himself on the baseball field.

We played Nashville in one of those silly exhibition games. We only got three guys hurt in that game. Randolph twisted his knee, Baylor pulled a hamstring, and Dale Murray scraped all the skin off his pitching toe because the mound was so crummy. I don't know why they schedule those exhibition games. As a player you don't have your heart in them a hundred percent because you know it doesn't count in the standings, and therefore, when you're not trying a hundred percent, you don't go all out, and that's how you get hurt.

On the other hand the game may prove to be one of the best things ever to happen to Nashville. We were beating them four to nothing going into the ninth, and they came up with five runs. Here's a bunch of kids losing to the New York Yankees, and they come back and beat us! And those kids were as happy as if they had won the World Series. They were giving high-fives all over the field. I had worked out, but Billy told me I didn't have to play, and I sat there on the bench watching them celebrate, and I was happy for them. They beat our good pitchers. They beat Rudy May, who's been around fifteen years. A lot of times we call up a pitcher from A ball to pitch for us so we don't have to use up one of our pitchers. But those kids beat a proven veteran major league pitcher in the ninth inning. Most of those kids will never make it to the big leagues, but it'll be something they can look back to their whole life.

Billy was having trouble with the umpires all night one game against Texas, and a couple times he was right. I was involved. There were two outs and I was batting against Rick Honeycutt. I had two strikes, and Smalley tried to steal home.

I'm up there guarding the plate, trying to get the run in, and on the next pitch, I hear someone running down the line yelling, "Don't swing, Puff, don't swing," and I look up, and it's Smalley.

You never—I mean never—steal home with two strikes on the batter. You can get killed that way. The pitcher throws it over, you have to swing, otherwise it's strike three, and the inning is over. When I'm out in the field, and the runner is bluffing to steal home with two strikes, I yell, "Take it if you want it." What good's it going to do you if the pitcher throws a strike? I didn't

BALLS

want to hit Smalley, so I just stood there scratching my head. I didn't know what the heck was going on.

Smalley comes sliding across the plate, and he's safe, and the umpire, who was blocked by the catcher, calls him out. Billy came out and argued that—to no avail.

I later found out the reason he went with two strikes. An earlier pitch had been way inside and almost hit me—it was right under my chin—and everyone assumed it was a ball, but the ump had called it a strike, making the count one and two. The next pitch was called a ball, and so Zimmer, the third-base coach, thought the count was three and one when it was really two and two.

A couple innings later, I was on first base, and I was running, and there was a grounder to second, and I came sliding in just as the shortstop was about to make the relay, and I threw a shoulder into him. He was right on the base, and I had the right to do that, and the umpire called an automatic double play. Billy came out and argued that.

And then later in the game, a Texas player hit a ball that we thought bounced over the fence, which should have been a double, but the umpire said it hadn't bounced. The ump may have been right on that, but Billy argued that one too.

And then the next inning Billy stood in the dugout with his cap turned sideways, and before I knew it, the umpire called time and looked into the dugout and pointed at Billy. Billy came out of the dugout, and the ump screamed, "If you don't turn your hat around, I'm throwing you out of here." Billy screamed, "I can wear my hat any way I want." The ump said, "That's it. You're out

43

of here. You're gone.'' And then Billy started kicking dirt on him.

As he was leaving the dugout, Billy ordered all our starting pitchers who weren't going to play that day to wear their hats sideways. And they sat that way the rest of the game. I really didn't know you could be thrown out of a game for wearing a hat sideways. Earl Weaver used to wear it backwards when he went out and argued. Maybe you can wear it backwards but not sideways.

The fact is that a lot of the players think that the umps are getting on Billy because of the Yankee ad campaign that features pictures of Billy kicking dirt on an umpire. Everyone knows George rehired Billy because he draws fans, and before the season started, he made these posters, and the yearbook shows the same picture, and it's only going to make it tough on us.

The second game of the season, Billy told the press, "I'm declaring war on the umpires." Hell, that doesn't do the players any good. It just makes it tougher to do our jobs when the umps are against us. But that's the way Billy likes to do things. Plus the fact that any time a play is called against us, George gets tapes and sends them to the league office to prove how the umpires are wrong. So the umps are going to have a hard-on for us all the time, which makes it that much tougher. We can't say anything to anyone. Billy isn't going to change. He's been successful doing it his way. I don't think the umps would consciously screw us, because they have a lot of integrity, but if it's a close call, all this is not going to influence them in our favor either.

My second big league at bat I was standing at home plate. Ed Runge was the home plate ump. I walked up to hit. While the catcher was out on the mound talking to the pitcher, Runge said to me, "You're from San Diego, aren't you?" I said, "Yeah." He said, "San Diego High?" I said, "Yeah." His son had been there a couple years ahead of me. He said, "Good luck to you. I'm pulling for you guys from San Diego, especially San Diego High, to make it." I said, "Thanks a lot, Ed. I appreciate it." Joel Horlen was the pitcher, and the first pitch he threw me was a curve outside, which the catcher caught on a bounce almost. Runge went, "Strike one." I didn't say anything, because I had heard you don't say anything to Ed Runge, because he likes to test rookies. I just stood there. The next pitch I figured Horlen was going to throw outside, so I was leaning way out, and he threw it inside and it must have had six inches of the plate, and Runge says, "Ball one." From then on, when Runge was behind the plate, I had a very small strike zone, and he was an umpire pitchers ordinarily loved. Six inches from the plate either way was a strike, usually. But he gave me pitches like no other umpire. Because I didn't complain to him when he tested me.

It taught me a lesson right there—not to give umpires a lot of grief. And I never have. I tell the young players coming up, "Don't give the umpires crap. Don't say anything. Accept the calls, because in the long run you'll get the breaks."

Billy was suspended for three games. George certainly had a lot of guys to pick from to take his place. I thought maybe they were going to call up Johnny Oates, the Columbus manager. I asked Torborg, "Is Oatsie coming up for three days?" He says, "Nah. We'll just use one of the guys we got." I said, "You're the logical guy, Jeff. You have the longest contract." He has a six-year contract. I don't know how they decided on Zimmer. They could have brought back Gene Michael from his scouting or even Lem, who's still getting paid by George. Or Clyde King.

I assumed Billy would be on the phone calling in, but we haven't heard a word from him. Zim has done a good job, but we haven't scored any runs. Zim hasn't messed up. I would like to play for him. He can tell who's giving a hundred percent out there. He knows the game. And he's not afraid to admit that he's made a mistake. If I'm running the bases and I come into third, I'll say, "I shouldn't have tried that. They should have had me," and he'll say, "Oh, no. I was waving you over. I was just as much at fault as you were." A lot of coaches, when you give them an out, will take it. I like guys who can admit they made a mistake.

Zim is a tough little guy. When he was playing with the Dodgers he was hit with a fastball in the temple, and the doctors had to put a plate in his head. He took a lot of heat when he was managing Boston. They booed him a lot, and he just kept going out there. He was man enough to do it. A lot of managers might send their pitching coach out. Not Zim. He told me, "I'll go out and do it. If they're going to boo me, they're going to boo me."

One day the radio in my locker was getting a lot of interference. I asked him to move his locker away from mine. I said, "It must be you, Zim. The plate in your head is messing up my radio."

Toward the end of the month, we were playing in Texas, and George called a team meeting and went over all the negative statistics. It was a very negative meeting.

We were in the clubhouse before the game, and suddenly the coaches started yelling: "Meeting. Get in here. We're going to have a meeting." We went into the manager's office, and there was George, standing there with Billy, and we were all sitting around in the office, and George started going over everyone individually, telling us how bad we were going. We don't need anyone to tell us that we're going bad. We know we are. But he always likes to point out the negative aspects of the game rather than the positives.

Like he told me, "Graig, you're hitting .080 with men in scoring position." It was a ridiculously low figure. Then he said, "And you've hit into five double plays." He said, "You have to stop doing that." But how do you keep from hitting into a double play? I felt like telling him, "Tell the guy in front of me to stop getting on first base, and I won't hit into any more double plays." It verges on the criminal to put that sort of thought into the mind of a player, because every time you get up with men on base, you start thinking, "My God, the owner doesn't want me to hit into a double play. I better be careful." And you can't hit with thoughts like that in your head.

That night I hit into another double play. As I was running down to first base, I was thinking to myself, "My

47

God, another double play. George's computer is going crazy.''

He has us plugged into computer baseball. He's got numbers, statistics, statistics, and numbers. But what he doesn't seem to realize is that the computer doesn't give an accurate picture. The night before we had been beaten by Texas. We had hit line drives all over the ballpark that were caught, and they hit bloop base hits over third, over first, and they beat us with the bloops. But all George saw was the bottom line, and so he told us how much better Texas was than we were that night, when actually we knew that though we hit the ball better, they were just luckier that night. His computer doesn't show that.

It doesn't show when a batter moves a runner over from second to third with nobody out. All it shows is that you've failed to hit with a man in scoring position. But these are the kinds of subtleties he doesn't understand, because he is the bottom-line man.

He went and told the relief pitchers how lousy they've been doing. He had a new statistic on them: If you come into the game with a man on base, and the man scores, you get a minus one. If he doesn't score, you get a plus one. But that doesn't take into consideration a situation such as a relief pitcher coming in with a man on third and nobody out. The batter hits a grounder or a fielder makes an error, allowing the runner to score. He's done his job, and yet he gets a minus one. There are so many variables that he hasn't taken into consideration with this.

George was the only one speaking at the meeting. Billy sat there and took it all in. I felt really bad for Billy, because that's not Billy's type of meeting. Billy holds meetings that end on a positive note.

George said he was going to discuss things like he would at a corporate meeting. In fact, he said, "If you guys were working for one of my other corporations, you'd all be fired right now." And then he came out with all the statistics. He said, "I've tried to get rid of all of you, but nobody wants you because you're all making too much money."

He just tries to make you feel bad. He tries to intimidate people. And there are too many veteran players here who don't need to be intimidated. They just need to be left alone. We know what to do. If you just keep playing the game every day, you come out of these things. It was a little early in the season to panic, I thought. But that's the way the owner runs his business. And he said he was going to run the Yankees the same way.

Billy sat there and listened, and there wasn't much he could do. Billy even let him make a lineup switch. That day George wanted Wynegar to catch instead of Cerone. During the game Billy told me in the dugout, "I really feel bad about myself letting George do that to me. I won't let him do it again. But I had to do it to appease him so he'll stay off you players." What Billy did might have been for the good of the team, but Billy felt really awful about it.

4

1969—1974

I got to Cleveland in 1969, and that was the year George Steinbrenner almost bought that team from the Stouffers. Way back I was almost playing for George, but at the last minute Stouffer refused to sell him the team.

Cleveland was the type of place where everybody was thrilled if we finished at five hundred. I had just come from a winning team—the Twins had won our division by nine games—and to come over to a club happy to be playing five hundred ball was depressing. The only good thing was that I was finally getting a chance to play every day, and that enabled me to show the rest of the league that I was a major league third baseman. I was grateful to have gotten that opportunity.

When you play on a team like Cleveland, what you're trying to do more than anything else is to impress other general managers. There's no point playing for the team, especially when everyone's happy at five hundred. You also are trying to impress the other players. There is nothing selfish about it. You try your hardest. What you're doing is trying to say, "Look at me. I'm a good player. Make a deal for me." About all you can hope for playing for Cleveland is to impress other general managers, and I guess I did that. I guess I impressed the Yankees' Lee MacPhail and Ralph Houk, because they made the trade that got me over to the Yankees. So it worked out perfect for me. In Cleveland, I got my chance to establish myself, and then after three years, I moved on to a contender.

It was frustrating playing in that big ballpark in Cleveland with eighty thousand seats and having only five thousand people in them. We'd have a big crowd opening day, but Cleveland was a town that was living in the past. Always they would refer to the 1948 Indians, blah blah blah: "We drew two million six in 1948, blah, blah, blah." Everyone said what a great baseball town Cleveland was, but we players couldn't see it. What else was there to do in 1948 but go to a ballgame? There was no television. It was right after the war. Everyone was happy. Even people living in downtown Cleveland. By the time I got there in 1970, the downtown was run down, and the ballpark was crummy, dingy, and old, and it couldn't have been much fun for the people to come to the game.

Management never hassled the players, as it does in New York, but everything was so low-budget. We had a third-base coach, Bobby Hoffman, who was also our traveling secretary. We used to get on Bobby, tease him about his having one set of signals for the players and another set for the bus driver. Sometimes he would get confused, and the bus driver would steal second base and the players would load the gear onto the bus.

BALLS

The Indians were so cheap that when we'd fly, say from Cleveland to New York, on the day of the game, we would always fly by charter after 12:01 in the afternoon to save a half day's meal money. Gabe was always trying to save a few dollars here and a few dollars there.

The only high-salaried player they had on that team was Ken Harrelson. They had just gotten him from Boston. Harrelson's career went into decline when he came to the Indians. He was out of his element in Cleveland. He had a big ego, and he needed a place like New York or Chicago or Boston for his stage. He broke his leg about halfway through that first year, and then Chris Chambliss was called up to take his place, and Harrelson never made it back after that.

I went to New York after the 1972 season. Gabe traded me and Gerry Moses for Charlie Spikes, Rusty Torres, Jerry Kenny, and John Ellis. New York needed a third baseman, and Cleveland needed some bodies. At that time it looked like a good trade for both teams. I was happy coming to New York, and I liked it even better that New York didn't have to give up anybody who had been a big part of their success in '72. They had won ninety-two games, and the only regular they gave up was Jerry Kenny, and he wasn't any great shakes. I figured we had a real shot to win the pennant in '73, and I was very happy.

I was happy just to play for Ralph Houk. I had heard many good things about him. Ralph ranks right up there among the two or three best managers I ever played for (I'm only counting Billy once even though he's been my manager four times). Ralph was so easy to get along with. He was tough if he had to be. If a player came into his office and started yelling, he'd close the door and challenge him to a fight. He did that to Mike Kekich one time. Mike wanted to know why he wasn't pitching, and he asked Ralph at the wrong time, and Ralph just walked over and slammed the door and challenged him to a fight.

Ralph was great for the players. I remember the all-star break that year. You get three days off, and some managers want you working out. Ralph said, "Goddammit, I don't want to see any of you sonsabitches for three days. Just get out of here, leave the country, do what you want to do, but get out of here." He treated the players with respect. He never ripped them in the press.

When I arrived, the Yankee management consisted of Ralph, Lee MacPhail, the general manager, and Mike Burke, who was president. And then one month after I was traded from Cleveland, George Steinbrenner bought the team. I didn't know who George Steinbrenner was. I had just spent three years in Cleveland, and I still never heard of the guy. Then he bought the club, and we learned that he was a ship builder and that he had promised not to interfere with the club, and then he kicked Mike Burke out, and Lee MacPhail quit, and he bothered Ralph so badly that Ralph ended up quitting.

Things were strange on the Yankees from the first spring training. I had been there only a couple weeks when two of our pitchers, Fritz Peterson and Mike Kekich, told us they had swapped families, wives, kids, dogs, and station wagons. I had never heard of such a thing. It was the first of the circuslike happenings. And the season hadn't even started.

Then George got into the act. At opening day at Yankee Stadium, we were lining up for the national anthem, and from his box George wrote down the uniform numbers of players whose hair he felt was too long. The next day in the clubhouse Ralph Houk called us to come around him, and he read a letter from Steinbrenner. Ralph said, "Okay, now the following players have to get haircuts." And Ralph read off the uniform numbers, "Number 28, number 19, number 41." We were laughing like hell, and Ralph really built it up. Every time he announced a number, we roared. It was so funny. Steinbrenner owned the team, and he didn't even know the names of his players.

But after that, to Ralph nothing much was funny. Ralph hates when anyone interferes with his running the ballclub, and George kept leaving him messages and calling up on the phone, driving him crazy, and Ralph got so upset he finally quit. Ralph didn't need to take that crap from somebody like George. Who was George? He had had no previous experience in baseball. What did he know about running a baseball team? And instead of trying to make an old pro like Ralph happier, George was trying to piss him off every chance he got. And by the end of the year, Burke was gone, and MacPhail was gone, and Ralph was gone, and George was in control of everything. Once George saw what a good deal he had put together, he started buying out the other guys who came in with him, and soon he ran the show, all by himself.

I must say, in June of that first year under George,

something happened that did make me very happy. This was before free agency, remember, and at that time it was rare that a team bought a star from another team in the middle of the season. Under Burke and MacPhail the Yankees had pinched nickels the whole time. What happened was that George bought both Sam McDowell and Pat Dobson in two separate deals. It cost him a couple hundred grand.

Ralph said to me, "This owner is giving me a lot of trouble so far with all these phone calls, but one thing about him, he isn't afraid to spend some money and buy some players when we need them." Ralph loved that, and so did I, because I had just come from Cleveland where they would never have made a move like that. In Cleveland they were worried most about saving a dollar. In New York, it was "Spend as much as you can." I like that aspect of George, that he wants to win so badly that he'll go out and do whatever he can to make us a winner. And that's all any player can ask for. So I was very impressed when he got Sudden Sam and Dobber.

But Ralph kept complaining that George was calling him on the phone all the time. He'd call during the game, in the middle of the night. Things he's done to all his managers since. Ralph had never had to put up with that from an owner before. George was telling him who to play, what to do. Ralph would pick up the phone in the dugout during a game, and George would be on the other end. It still goes on.

Despite what Ralph told me about George, I didn't realize the problems were as bad as they were until the final day of the season. The final game didn't mean anything, and after the game, the guys were getting ready to go home. But the word was, "Stay around until the end of the game. Ralph is going to make an announcement." I didn't know what it was going to be. And at the end of the game, you could hear the fans outside in the stadium, tearing the stadium apart, because it was the last game in Yankee Stadium for two years while they renovated, and with all that noise going on outside, in the clubhouse underneath the stands, here was Ralph Houk telling us that he was leaving.

As we sat around on the stools by our lockers, Ralph came out and said, "I got to tell you guys something. I've had enough. I'm quitting." And he broke down into tears.

I spoke to him afterward and Ralph said, "I have to quit before I hit the guy." Ralph said, "I don't want to leave the game of baseball by punching an owner. But if he keeps on bothering me like he does, I'll end up hitting him."

What could I say? Good luck. My car was outside the stadium, all packed. I got in, and I drove home to San Diego. I was by myself. Sitting in the car driving across the country I was screaming: "Why the hell did this have to happen? I finally get a manager I really like and respect, and the goddamn owner forces him out. Why did this have to happen?" Looking back, we've had a different manager almost every year. But as I was driving west, I desperately wished for things to be different. Ralph had put the deal together to get me from Cleveland. Once, when I was with the Indians, Ralph came out onto the field to argue and as he was walking by, he said, "Boy, I'd like to have you on my team." He had been the one who wanted me to play for him. I wish Ralph had stayed around a few more years.

Every time a manager gets fired, no matter how important a player you are, you have to be wondering, "Who's the manager going to be, and how will he treat me?" Before the next spring training, it was announced that Bill Virdon was going to manage. I didn't know him. He was a National League guy. Managed Pittsburgh. If you're going to get a manager, why bring in a guy from the National League? George had tried to get Dick Williams from Oakland, but the A's owner was Charley Finley and Finley wouldn't let him go unless George traded him two young minor leaguers, Scott McGregor and Otto Velez. George said, "You can't have McGregor because he's one of our crown jewels. He's going to be a Yankee forever. And besides, we need him later to get Ken Holtzman." So Virdon came over, and Virdon worked our asses off in spring training. It was the hardest camp I had ever attended. He ran us so much. He forced us to hit against the batting machines. He just made us hit, hit, hit, run, run, run. That was the way they had done it in Pittsburgh. When the season opened, we were in great shape. We had an excellent team. We had Thurman at his best, and Murcer, Sparky, Mel Stottlemyre, the Alou brothers, Doc Medich, and Virdon did an excellent job with that team. Virdon had the guts to take Bobby Murcer from center field and put Elliott Maddox out there, not a popular move because Murcer was the Golden Boy of New York. But Virdon, who had been a center fielder himself, saw Murcer play there a few times and said, "This is not going to be good enough," so he moved

Bobby to right and installed Maddox in center. I admired him for having the guts to make that move. And so did the pitchers.

And it was a fun team. That was the age when Sparky Lyle kept sitting nude on cakes. It was a loose clubhouse. We had characters. Dobson was a funny guy, Sparky too. Baseball was a lot more fun before free agency. Nobody was making the really big bucks. At that time the top players were making a hundred thousand dollars. Once free agency came in and the money went up, the pressure went up too. It took a lot of the fun out of the game. We used to fool around a lot, play hockey in the old clubhouse in Yankee Stadium. Some of those guys would come out of there bloody. Now you're afraid to do it because it might cost you a million dollars on the free agent market if you're injured. In those days, you took your chances. You didn't care all that much, because there wasn't the big money to be made.

And we played good, team ball and were successful, even though we were a team without a home. We were playing in Shea Stadium, where nobody liked to play. We were in a real small clubhouse. Murcer had a particularly hard time. He didn't hit a home run over there until the final game. He had such trouble. We all did. We would take the field before the game, and we'd be booed. The Mets fans were coming to the games. The true Yankee fans wouldn't even go over there to watch us. They waited the two years for us to come back to the stadium. It was like we were on the road for two years.

But despite having to play there, we went down to the final two days of the 1974 season before we lost.

* * *

We could see George slowly taking over the ballclub, buying out many of the partners. And then, after solidifying his power, he got suspended by Bowie Kuhn for two years, which led to one of the funniest things I had ever seen as a player. That spring Virdon came into the clubhouse, and he was carrying a cassette recorder with him. George had sent a tape recording to play for us, to fire us up. He probably thought we were going to take that seriously, as though he were Knute Rockne giving his players a pep talk. He couldn't understand that we were sitting there at our lockers laughing at him. Damn, that was funny. Virdon didn't like to do it, but he was told to, so he did it, and so we were all laughing, and Virdon said, "Okay guys, you gotta listen to this." It was George giving us one of his rah rah speeches. No one could look anyone else in the face. We all turned toward our lockers to keep from breaking up laughing. We couldn't believe it. We had never heard anything like this! It was so strange. Virdon stood there with his stone face, trying to keep from being disrespectful, while we all sat in our lockers howling with laughter.

At the start of that meeting Virdon came out of his office, and lying on the floor sound asleep was a pitcher by the name of Mike Wallace. Mike used to live pretty hard. He lived in Manhattan, and so we called him Manhattan Mike, and this was a morning game, and he was dead asleep on the clubhouse floor, and Virdon had to step over him to give his speech and play George's tape recording. Wallace's days were numbered after that. Virdon was a no-nonsense guy. He didn't like the kind of life Wallace was leading.

At the end of April 1974, Gabe Paul, who had come

over with George from Cleveland, traded Peterson, Beene, Kline, and Buskey, the whole pitching staff, off to Cleveland. That was one trade that wasn't real popular with the players. I didn't like it. We were giving up half our pitching staff, guys who had been with the Yankees so long they were part of the family. We got quality players in Chambliss and Dick Tidrow, but it was still a shock. Virdon didn't know anything about it either. He was shocked that night too. They didn't consult him, and I don't think he would have approved. You just don't give away four of your pitchers right after spring training.

But as it turned out, it was one of the best deals Gabe made, because all those pitchers came up with sore arms, and both Chambliss and Tidrow became stars for us.

But at the time everyone was complaining about the Cleveland connection. George was from Cleveland, Gabe was from Cleveland, and so were Chambliss, Tidrow, Stanley, Upshaw, and myself. Cleveland had been a last-place team. Why would the fans want us dealing with Cleveland?

In other deals Gabe got Rudy May and Larry Gura, and we played great in August, and we won most of our games in September, but Baltimore was rolling right along with us, and they just wouldn't lose.

What really cost us was a fight between Bill Sudakis and Rick Dempsey in the lobby of a hotel in Milwaukee during the final days of the season. Sudakis had been on Dempsey pretty much that year, nagging him about little things, and bragging about what a great fighter he was. And Dempsey was upset that he was the second-string catcher, even though he knew Munson was a better catcher. Still, he wanted to play.

Sudakis was Mr. Macho. I guess he was a tough guy where he came from, 'cause he was always talking about all the fights he had. We never saw him fight, until that day. Suds was a strange guy. He had come from the National League, from the Dodgers, and players who come from the National League have an arrogance about them, an attitude that everything's done better in the National League. Suds thought he should be playing third base or catching or playing first base.

As the players were coming into the lobby of the hotel in Milwaukee, Dempsey suddenly turned and cold-cocked Sudakis, just let him have it. He dropped Sudakis. And then everyone ran in to break it up, and Bobby Murcer, who was one of our leading hitters, decided to play big referee, and he ended up getting stepped on and broke his hand. Here we were, battling for a pennant and in the last series of the year, and here's the team brawling in Milwaukee.

Sudakis was going crazy. He was stomping through the halls looking for Dempsey. All he had ever talked about was how tough he was, and the only time we ever saw him fight he got his ass kicked. In a small way, it was kind of humorous.

It was the next-to-last day, a Saturday, when we lost the '74 pennant. We still had a meaningless final game to play on Sunday, and George came into the clubhouse that Sunday in Milwaukee and gave us another of his rah rah speeches. He started by blaming our losing on Ralph Houk, who had moved over to Detroit. He said, ''I know

Baltimore won last night. Ralph Houk let them win. Ralph pitched a bunch of young kids so Baltimore would win." George never could accept defeat. There had to be someone to blame, so he blamed Ralph. Which didn't set too well with the Yankee players, who still adored Ralph. He couldn't admit that Baltimore had played one game better.

And instead of his saying, "You guys gave everything you had. Nice going. It was an incredible accomplishment, and I'm proud of you," he told us, "Today's game is the most important game of your career."

We all looked at one another, thinking, "What the hell is he talking about?" We had just battled 161 games and lost by one. George said, "You have to show the people of New York that you can go out a winner." For some reason, he thought the fans would hate us if we lost that last game, would think of us as quitters. He doesn't give the average fan very much credit. And he still hasn't learned, because he did the same thing after we lost the Series in '81. The fans are a lot smarter than he ever gives them credit for.

5

MAY 1983

I'm off to my best start in quite a few years as far as my average is concerned, but am not driving in many runs. Nobody is. The whole club is struggling. It's not something we talk about, but everyone is trying a little too hard, trying to do too much, instead of just relaxing, having fun, and playing ball.

Billy held a team meeting and said, "Stop pressing. Just do the job you're capable of doing, and everything will work itself out." I know the guys listen, and yet, when you get up to the plate, your own thoughts go through your mind, and you decide you don't want to leave it up to the next guy.

When you press, you say to yourself, "I have to do everything myself, because no one else is doing anything. If I can get hot, then I can carry the club, and we'll win more games." But the game of baseball doesn't work that way. To win you usually need three or four guys hitting at the same time. If I get on a hot streak, I could carry the club for a week or two, but my hot streaks come when I'm relaxed and swinging easy, not when I'm going out trying to carry the club.

Because everyone's pressing, especially with men on base, we have not been coming up with the big hits when we need them.

You have to say to yourself, "Over the course of the season, we're going to have slumps," and you have to be able to accept that. Our slump has lasted almost a month. We're hoping it's been because of the cold weather. Maybe when it warms up, the big hitters, Winfield and Baylor and Kemp, will warm up a bit too. But so far things haven't jelled. We haven't jelled as a team. We had it together during spring training, but once the season started, things didn't work out, and they haven't worked out yet.

Neither Baylor nor Kemp are hitting much at all. They know they're going bad. Baylor is hitting .300, but he hasn't driven in many runs, and Kemp is going as bad as anyone. Kemp'll admit it. He'll say, "I'm going as horseshit as anyone," but all he can do is keep trying. We have enough veteran guys that you can see that no one is going to give up. We're only three games out of first place, so actually, in that respect, everyone has a positive attitude.

What's alarming about our slump is that we're losing to the teams we should be beating. When we were dominating the league in the late seventies, we would kill the Rangers, the Twins, the White Sox. And now we're breaking even or they're beating us. These are the teams, when you look at the schedule you figure, "My gosh, this is the time to make hay and get off to a good start." And we've gotten off to a crummy start. Who knows what's going to happen when we play the big teams like Milwaukee, Boston, Baltimore? We better be out of our hitting slump. If we play like this all year, we're not going to be anywhere near the top. On paper we should have as good a team as anybody. But on the field is where we have to do it. We don't know what kind of character this team has. What kind of heart it has. That'll come through in the dog days of August. That's when we'll find out if we really have a good team.

Part of the problem may well be that we have new guys every year. But the new guys have fit in very well—Baylor and Kemp and Shirley. There are no conflicts, no petty jealousy. The new players have made a very smooth transition. And yet, our chemistry isn't right. There isn't the camaraderie on this team that we used to have.

After the game, you don't see many groups of four or five guys going out together. It's usually one or two who go off on their own. You can go out with anyone if you want to. There isn't a single prick on the club. Everyone's been around for so long, they have their own ways. They know what they want to do, where they want to go. On the road during the day I spend most of the time in my room. If I go into the hotel lobby, there are so many people to bother you it's really not worth it. If I don't stay in my room, I come out to the ballpark early and play cards.

At night I might walk into a bar, and there might be two of the other guys there. It's never ten or twelve guys. I hang out with Goose Gossage most of the time. We sit around and laugh. Piniella talks with Murcer, and I mean talks with him. Murcer will sit and listen for hours, and

Lou will talk about hitting or analyze the ballclub until your head starts to spin.

Piniella and Cerone get on Smalley about the way he dresses, about some of the strange-looking outfits he wears. I told the guys I had spent my off day in Minnesota going through department stores looking at mannequins to see how Smalley was going to be dressed the next day. He wears his shirt collars up and his sweaters slung over the shoulder. Piniella and Cerone tease him all the time, but he keeps wearing them, so it mustn't bother him too much.

Smalley still feels like an outsider, because he took a popular guy's job. He knows management isn't happy with him at shortstop. He knows they want to move him and get Robertson in there. I don't know yet if he's politicking for my job. I know he's got a good bat. And they're trying to find a position for him. When a guy can't make it at shortstop, the logical thing is to put him at third base or try him at first. The way things are with our pitching, a third baseman has to be quick, has to be able to leave his feet, to dive for the ball, and Roy won't do that because he has a bad shoulder. It's going to be hard for him to move me out at third. He can't play second. He can't DH because of Baylor. And he doesn't have the range to play shortstop. It remains to be seen what they end up doing with him. If he hadn't had his appendix out in spring training, he probably would have been the first baseman. Griffey has done okay at first. He's a lot better than I thought he was going to be. But Griffey's making a million a year. If Roy plays first, what are they going to do with Griffey?

There are rumors that Smalley would be traded to

Chicago for Dennis Lamp. We hear them. I don't know how it affects Roy. He doesn't talk about it. There is also a rumor that I was going to be traded to San Diego, but I know that's impossible, because I have a clause in my contract that I can't be traded unless I okay it. Rumors are usually just rumors. Another rumor going around the clubhouse is that Jerry Mumphrey is going to be traded. Jerry has asked out, and they told him that they are going to trade him, so that could happen any day now. Jerry has been here a couple years, does his job, hits .300 every year, but Billy doesn't want a center fielder who's the quiet and shy type. Billy wants someone aggressive, to take charge out there, and he doesn't feel that Mumphrey is that type of guy. I really can't see why Billy should be down on the guy. The papers keep saying he has a weak throwing arm, but that isn't true. His arm is fine. No complaints there. Maybe someone else is down on him and passed the word down to Billy. Maybe Billy saw him at a bad time and just got down on him. I don't know. But Jerry has gotten moved around in the shuffle here. For his sake, I hope he does get traded, because he's a real good guy, I really like him, and he deserves better.

As a player, I get very upset when I see someone like Jerry get treated the way he's been treated. But there's nothing you can do about it. And you don't want to take sides. That's how ballclubs start falling apart. The press will come up to you, asking what you think of his situation, and the best thing you can do is just stay out of it. But personally, you hate to see a guy get shit on for no apparent reason. The only reason is that the owner went out and signed so many quality outfielders that somebody's got to sit. You can only play three of them, and the others, who are used to playing every day, are going to be unhappy sitting down, no matter how much money they're making.

We have to play Winfield, we have to play Kemp, we have to play Griffey, we have to play Mumphrey, we have to play Oscar, we have to play Piniella. And that leaves Murcer singing his songs. Murcer's a country and western singer now. I've heard his song, "Skoal Dipping Man"—too many times. He got to play for us the other day against Oakland. Bobby was leading off, and he popped up, and when he came back to the bench he said, "In my prime I would have hit that ball in the upper deck." I said, "Bobby, that pitcher never heard of you as a player. He thinks you're another country and western singer." Bobby's in limbo right now. He's expecting any day to get released. It looks like he's going to be a radio and TV announcer with the Yankees.

Too many guys get caught in the numbers game on this team. Take Roger Erickson, for example. He's been in the big leagues four, five years. He pitched well in spring training, but there wasn't a spot for him. George's philosophy is to pay guys, and then if he doesn't use them, they serve as an insurance policy in the minors at Columbus. The player, however, doesn't want to be that insurance policy. He wants to be somewhere in the majors where he can pitch. It's a sad situation when a pitcher like Roger ends up at Columbus. I wish they would trade guys like that. You can't win pitching in the minors. If you are successful, they say, "You're a major league pitcher. You should win." If you get hit hard, they say, "You're washed up." It's an absolute no-win situation.

Also, and perhaps more important, a guy like that is taking the spot of a kid who should be there.

The other thing we do is jerk guys around, bouncing them back and forth between Columbus and New York. We have a large rookie first baseman by the name of Steve Balboni. A very easygoing guy. A couple of years ago I nicknamed Balboni The Mute, because when he came up, he sat around and didn't say a word. As long as they brought him up, I hoped that they would put him in the lineup and leave him there for three or four weeks and see what he could do. Instead he comes up with us, sits a couple of weeks, and goes back. Last year he was up and down so much that he ended up leading the International League in home runs, but he couldn't make the all-star team because he wasn't playing there long enough. "How did Bones do last night?" "He hit two home runs." I hope they give the guy a chance. He can play. But where? How could Billy juggle him in at first along with Griffey, Roy, and the other young kid, Mattingly?

We just have too much juggling going around out there. It's no wonder we don't have any consistency. But I don't know any other way to do it. Trade some of them and get some pitching. I know George wouldn't just sell them. He doesn't need the money. But I can't see us going through the whole year with so much talent sitting one day and playing the next.

We've played thirty games and have had thirty different lineups. That's one of the problems. If we could play with a set lineup, we'd be so much better off. In 1978, when we made our big comeback, we were just getting over injuries, and we had a set lineup the last two months of the season, and that made a big difference.

It's impossible for the Yankees to have a set lineup this year because the owner has gotten us too many good players. And even if Billy could pick eight guys and let them play, right now I don't know which players he would pick. He probably doesn't either. Nobody's real hot right now. So Billy keeps juggling them, hoping somebody gets hot, hoping the team gets on a streak, and then he'd have a reason to stay with a set lineup.

Goose was on the mound in Kansas City, and there was a runner on first who would have beaten us if he had gotten around to score. When Goose gets involved in the game, he forgets all about the runners on base. He goes into the stretch without giving them a look. I walked over to the mound and told him, "Give the guy a look over to first." He went into his stretch and didn't look, and the guy got a great jump and would have stolen second easily, but the batter fouled the ball off. I went over to Goose again. He had the rosin bag in his hand, and he slammed it down onto the mound. He started screaming and yelling at me. He said, "Get off my mound. Get back to your position. Get off my ass. Stop bothering me. I've been doing this for thirteen years, so just stop bothering me."

I threw my hands up in disgust and walked back to my position. He got the next guy out and saved the game for us. I was really upset after the game. I said, "Don't ever show me up like that on the field, Goose.'' He and I are best of friends, but it took me an hour after the game to calm down about it. The players were joking about it. They wanted to know if we were still going to sit together on the plane. Was this a breakup? It was funny after a while, but at the beginning I was really hot. He apologized right after the game as we were walking up the runway, but I was still pretty angry.

The fans in the stands could see us. It was in Kansas City, and they were roaring. They were loving it. It's rare that ballplayers get upset with one another. Teammates have great respect for one another. Everyone has had the same problems coming up. Everyone knows that things won't be right every day, so you bear with them.

I make it a practice never to get angry with a pitcher for not doing the job, for hanging a slider, because you don't want him to get angry with you when you make an error. The only pitcher I've ever been mad at during my entire career was Ed Figueroa. He was having trouble with George and didn't want to pitch. He said, "When I go out there, I'm just going to throw the ball over and let them hit it.'' That made me angry. The guy wasn't trying. He felt he was being shit on, he wanted out of New York, so he didn't give his best when he was on the mound, until the Yankees finally got rid of him.

When things didn't start to pick up, Dave Winfield called a team meeting at which everyone had a say as to what they thought was wrong. We sat in the players' lounge and bullshitted for about fifteen minutes. Anyone who had any gripes aired them, and we talked about why we weren't winning. You'd have thought we were ten, not three, games out. It's just that George drums his "win, win, win" into everybody, so if we're not in first place by May, everyone starts to get nervous. Not because of the reality of the standings, but because of the reality of George's expectations. I really thought it was a little early for a meeting like that.

The players have a tendency to panic without extra pressure. They believe what they read in the papers, which is their first mistake. They listen to George and they think that we're going to be blown out of the pennant race in the first two months of the season! I think all this rah rah stuff isn't necessary. Over a six-month schedule, the best team is going to win, whether you hold one meeting a year or a hundred meetings a year. These meetings accomplish zero.

When they asked me what I thought, I said, "Just go out and have fun." I said, "You guys have fun in batting practice, and you hit well in batting practice. So why not go out with the same attitude during the game? If you get a base hit, that's great. But if you've done your best and make an out, that's all right too. Don't worry about the fat man upstairs coming down on you. Just go out and have fun. Pretend it's batting practice, and quit reading all the negative statistics." A statistics sheet comes into the clubhouse every day, and it shows what everybody's hitting with men in scoring position. Nobody was doing much. I said, "Don't concern yourself if you're hitting .100 with men in scoring position because that's such a bullshit statistic anyway. And if you don't like what's being written about you in the papers, quit reading them."

Ignoring the press is easier said than done. Someone has been planting negative things about me in the papers. And it bothers me. If a writer wants to say I made an error or I failed to drive in a run, fine. But a writer shouldn't write that "Graig Nettles can't do it anymore," just because I made one error. In one game I was lousy, and the writers started saying I can't play anymore. I went and asked Billy. I said, "I read in three different newspapers how shitty I'm playing third base." Billy was taken aback. He said, "What the hell are they talking about? You're playing great third base." I said, "I thought I was too." I said to Billy, "Where is this negative talk coming from? Who's telling the reporters this? I'd like to know where it's coming from." Billy said, "It's not coming from me. And George hasn't even been around, so I don't think it's coming from upstairs. I don't know."

I don't know either. If certain newspaper people have it in for you, they're going to try to stab you in the back whenever they can. The *New York Post*'s Henry Hecht, for instance, has it in for me. We've had our share of arguments. And there was another guy, Mike Shalin, who worked for the *Post* last year, who was always trying to start controversy. I had a bad streak last year when I was making some errors, and he went around to some of my teammates to talk about how poorly I was playing. They wouldn't take the bait, so they didn't say anything, but when I found out about it, I had it out with him, told him what I thought of him. I said, "Don't ever talk to me again. And don't ever try to go behind my back and get my teammates to talk about me like that again." He just pretended he didn't know what I was talking about.

Still, Henry Hecht is the worst. He wrote that I had lost it. He once wrote that Guidry had lost it. If you mess up a play, he'll gladly write how poor you're doing, but if you make a great play—or three great plays—there'll be no mention of it. He's like a vulture eager to pounce on an erring ballplayer. He waits to pick you apart, and he can get away with it because he has the power of the press behind him. Guys like Hecht can do whatever they want. That's why I'm glad that in New York most of our games are televised, and the fans can actually see for themselves what's going on on the field. They don't have to take the word of a writer like Hecht.

The more controversy on the ballclub the *New York Post* can generate, the happier the people at the *Post* will be.

We don't discuss the reporters much, because that just makes us mad, but dumping a few of them in the whirlpool might not be a bad idea. Some reporters when they don't have a story will make one up. They make up anonymous quotes, and you wonder where they come from.

Are they coming from George? We wonder about that sometimes. It's like when Dick Young said, "Graig Nettles is a defensive liability at third base." Where is he getting that from? Is he getting that from the front office?

And I can't ask him, because he wouldn't tell me. He'd say, "Graig, that's just my opinion."

I'm having a good year. It's as good a year as I could have hoped for. Things are going along great. I'm playing fine in the field, and I'm hitting the ball harder than I have in my whole career, two, three, four times a game. Billy has shown a lot of confidence in me, moved me up into the middle of the lineup—I've even hit cleanup against right-handed pitchers a couple times. I'm third on the team in RBIs behind Winfield and Baylor, and second in home runs behind Winfield, and I'm very, very happy about it, because this is the time of year when I usually start hitting well. Right now, my average is the least of my worries. It's at .270 and, I hope, it'll go higher from here.

Henry Hecht finally got his due from Billy. Hecht had written an article about the team meeting that took place in Texas in April when George gave one of his rah rah speeches. Henry wrote that after George left the room, Billy told the players, "Don't pay any attention to what he said. I'm running this ballclub." And Henry Hecht wasn't even in Texas. It was simply untrue. Billy never said that. What really happened was that after George left, we were going over the hitters on the other team, and Billy said, "Don't worry about a lot of things. I'm managing the club on the field." But he never said, "Forget what that bleep said. I'm running the show." Hecht turned the words around to make it sound like Billy was berating George. So Billy got upset about that, and the next day called a team meeting with the press in the clubhouse, and he chewed Henry Hecht up one side and down the other.

In the clubhouse in front of the whole team and the rest of the reporters, Billy pointed to Hecht and said, "You see this little scrounge right here? This guy got me fired twice, and he's trying to get me fired again. Any of you guys who talk to this little scrounge," he kept referring to him as a scrounge, "any of you guys who talk to this little scrounge, don't talk to me." He said, "Henry, I won't stop you from making your living. You can come in the clubhouse, but don't try to come in my office. If you do, I'll dump you in the whirlpool. If you were a big enough man, I'd dump you right now. What do you think of that?" Henry said, "You can imagine what I think of you." Billy said, "Yeah, I know. I read the shit every day."

It was probably the best clubhouse meeting we ever had. After the meeting I said, "We finally had a clubhouse meeting that made some sense."

Afterward Henry Hecht went around and tried to talk to the guys. We told him, "Go away, Henry. I don't want to talk." To Henry's bizarre way of thinking, anyone who said "Go away" was talking to him. And the next day Henry wrote that ten guys had talked to him after Billy told them not to. We talked to him all right. We told him to keep away from us.

Henry then wrote an article, "Why the Yankees Are Going Nowhere," and in it he ripped Billy, said that George should fire him. The reason I saw the article was that the other reporter from the *Post*, Mike McAlary, came walking into the clubhouse in Detroit with it to make sure that everybody saw it. It's so perfect the way the *Post* works. I could hear Hecht telling McAlary, "Make sure you take that paper to Detroit and make sure it gets into the clubhouse so the players can see it so it can start some more shit."

One of the things Hecht's article said was that the reason Billy plays me at third and not Smalley is that "Nettles is probably one of Billy's few allies in pinstripes right now." This is Henry Hecht again taking shots at Billy. He's been doing that the whole time Billy's been here. And that's one reason I don't like Henry Hecht, because of the butcher job he did on Billy before.

We had a lot of laughs about Billy's tirade. Everyone was very happy about that, because there is no one on the ballclub who likes Henry Hecht, who is a scrounge just like Billy says. And what bothers me most about Henry is that he's the first one to blast a player, but if anyone dared criticize him, he would go crazy. Henry may only be four feet tall, but with a pen and a notebook, he's a bully, because he knows that there is no way to fight back. Everybody was glad to see him get chewed out in front of everybody.

I just hope the incident hasn't made Henry a folk hero.

The next day he was on all the radio talk shows, and I'm sure that's exactly what he wanted. The other writers, whether they like Henry Hecht or not, had to back him because he's a writer and Billy was attacking one of their fraternity members.

I don't have a good relationship with the *New York Post*. I told a writer from the *Los Angeles Times* that I would rather have my kids find a *Hustler* magazine around the house than a *New York Post*. Any time there's a controversy that I'm involved in, the *Post* is going to take the other side. I hope the fans of the city of New York are too sophisticated to believe a scandal sheet like the *Post*. At least the *National Enquirer* admits that it makes up some of its stories.

I can picture the *Post* editors sitting around a table, having their little clubhouse meetings at the paper, where the publisher says, "Try to stir up as much shit as you can."

Doyle Alexander is a very quiet guy. He never says a word. He doesn't seem to get upset about many things. It was very uncharacteristic of him to punch the dugout wall in Seattle last year and break his hand. It was the first time I ever saw him get upset.

George gave him a million a year for a couple years. I was surprised George gave him so much money. He isn't overpowering, throws a lot of slow stuff. If he doesn't have good control and get the ball down in the strike zone, he gets hit awfully hard. He was the pitcher George wanted two years ago, and he went out and got him.

And now George is on Doyle's back. In fact, George has been on everybody's back. When Shane was going bad, he said, "The deal for Shane Rawley last year was the worst deal I ever made." If Shane starts going great, George will say, "I knew all along he was going to be a good pitcher."

George is even on Goose's back. I'm feeling kind of down about Goose. Goose and I are the closest of friends, and he's in a slump right now. He's come in three or four times and hasn't gotten the job done. He's very frustrated. He'll throw a pitch, his usual ninety-mile-an-hour fastball, and the batter will hit it, bloop it, dink it, ping it, and you can see his frustration. He has a bewildered look on his face, like, "Why is this happening?" None of us can figure it out, because there is nothing wrong with his arm. I know he goes through these stretches, but it's so tough to have to watch him. Still, rather now than later in the season when the games are more crucial, when we could get blown out of a pennant race. We're only a game and a half out of first place. That's encouraging. Plus the fact that Goose is still throwing as hard as ever. From third base I can tell when a pitcher is losing his speed—that's about the only thing I can see—and he is throwing just as hard.

Goose has tried hard to keep his upper lip stiff. He's been very tough on himself, but he's trying to keep on an even keel until this thing blows over. Fortunately, off the field he doesn't punish himself. He doesn't take the game away from the field. That's why we get along so well together. We leave it in the ballpark. When we go out after the game, we don't talk much about baseball at all. It helps you keep your sanity.

But Goose has been down, and he felt even worse after George called Jerry Kapstein, who is both my agent and Goose's, and he read Kapstein the riot act about how badly Goose has been pitching. George told Kapstein, "For all the money I'm paying him, your man isn't doing shit."

Whatever Goose needs, he doesn't need that. Goose is such a tough guy, you wouldn't think George could get to him, but as Goose has said, with George you never know. At any moment he might on a whim make a deal. He did it with Dick Tidrow four years ago. He got upset with Tidrow because he gave up some home runs, and boom, he got rid of him right away, which proved to be a bad mistake. But he does these things, and for some reason, two springs ago, he wanted Doyle Alexander badly. I don't know why. But he did. We were all set to make a deal for Dave Stieb from Toronto, but out of the clear blue here comes George with all these ideas why he wanted Alexander. Later he tried to shift the blame to the coaches. But the coaches said, "No, George, that was your idea." Which it was. So you never know what goes on in the man's mind. Nobody's ever secure here, unless you have a no-trade clause or you're a ten and five man. That ten and five rule, which says a player in the big leagues for ten years and with one team for five cannot be traded without his permission, was one of the best things to happen to veterans. Once I got that, I knew they would have to come to me if they wanted to make a trade. They couldn't even start rumors about me. It's like the trade rumors with Cerone now. It's silly to even talk about it, because he has a no-trade clause in his contract.

Of course, because of all the turnover, George keeps a lot of guys from becoming ten and five players. A lot of guys get traded after their fourth year if they've been around a while. A lot of it has to do with the way they depreciate ballplayers for tax write-offs. They usually depreciate a guy for five years, and so you get rid of a guy after that fourth year and send him to another club so a new owner can start depreciating him for five years. There's a lot more to trading than ability on the field.

And yet, if you want a winning team, you have to have the same guys playing the same positions year after year. The Dodgers have proved that. Baltimore does that. For a long time we had Chambliss at first, Willie at second, Bucky at short, and me at third, and that stability helped us a lot, but then George got rid of Chambliss and Bucky. He wants to prove you can win by keeping everybody on edge.

Goose said that the players stopped pulling for one another after the 1981 World Series. He said the 1981 World Series left a bitter taste, and it did. I'll tell you when baseball stopped being a lot of fun: the final playoff game against Milwaukee in '81. We got off to a two-nothing lead in games in the series, and then they came back to New York and beat us two straight. After that fourth game, we got in the clubhouse, and there was George sitting in there, and he just started chewing us up one side and down the other. "What the hell are you people doing losing? How could you possibly lose two games in a row? If you lose tomorrow's game, you better look around the room, because a lot of you veteran players will be gone, and blah blah blah." Here we are, we fought all year long to get to the playoffs. We get there. It was the strike season, so we had been assured of the playoffs once the strike was over. We got to the play-offs, and here he is chewing us out for having the audac-ity to lose two games in a row. Everyone kind of looked at one another and said, "What the hell are we doing here? What fun is the game anymore if you get to the playoffs and still get chewed out by your owner?" That's when a lot of the fun stopped.

We went out and beat Milwaukee the next day and then went out and swept Oakland three straight, and then we won the first two games of the World Series, and then LA came back and beat us, and they beat us fair and square. And then George apologized to the fans of New York, which was degrading. They weren't expecting an apology. Our baseball fans are knowledgeable. They re-alize that there are twenty-six teams and that only two of them even get into the World Series and that only one of those two teams can win. There's no reason to apologize for being on the losing side. I could understand maybe if we had fallen down, hadn't given a good effort. But we gave a good effort, and they beat us. So why apologize?

Then he punished us by making us report to spring training three weeks early in 1982. After the '81 Series, it was never as much fun as it used to be. Goose is so right.

And in '82, we started the season with Bob Lemon, and he was there for a couple weeks, and then we had Gene Michael, and then Clyde King. And it became con-stant change, constant turmoil.

We try hard not to sit around the clubhouse and talk about George. It just causes irritation when we talk about the stuff that he does. Because you never get a pat on the back here, never "Nice going." It's always negative, and so when you bring him up, you're bringing up the negative part of the game. So we try not to.

When Willie Randolph got hurt, Billy put Andre at second for a few games. He did all right. We had a twenty-one-year-old kid, Don Mattingly, sitting on the bench, and he needed some playing time, so they sent him down to Columbus where he could play. Since Randolph was hurt, they decided to bring up an extra infielder, so they brought up Bert Campaneris. At age forty-one, he went four for five in his first game. So much for our youth movement.

I did an interview on cable TV the other night, and they asked me if I was surprised about the job Campaneris did. I said, "Not really, he's only a couple of years older than I am, and I expect to be doing the same thing in a couple of years. So it doesn't surprise me at all."

I admire Campy's dedication. He went to Mexico for a year, then tried out for the Yankees, and when he was cut in spring training, he could have said, "I'll go back and play in Mexico again." Instead he went to Columbus. He's been around long enough to know that breaks happen, and Willie's injury was the break that he needed to come back to the big leagues. When he got here, he said, "Billy, play me, I'm hot." He had gotten a couple of hits the night before at Columbus. Sure enough, he got hits his first four at bats.

After Randolph got hurt, we went to Texas, and after the first day Willie went back to New York to have his knee examined. We have to wear ties on the road, and Oscar Gamble was panicked because Randolph wasn't there to tie his tie for him. Oscar can't tie his own tie. Willie does it for him. "Goddamn it, where the hell is Willie when I need him?"

Oscar is a genuinely funny guy. When George gave us his talk about what we were hitting with men in scoring position, Oscar said, "Hell, when I'm hitting, I am in scoring position." A couple days ago, he was in the training room. He's had a sore shoulder. I was there stretching my legs. Bill Bergesch, the assistant general manager, came waddling in. I nicknamed Bergesch Dr. Gloom, because every time the ax has to fall, George sends him down to the clubhouse to bring the bad news. Dr. Gloom began talking to Oscar, asking how his shoulder was. Oscar says, "It's really feeling a lot better." Bergesch says, "It really feels all right?" Oscar says, "Yeah." Bergesch says, *"This time* we're really going to get you into the games. There's no bullshit *this time.* We're going to get you in." When I heard that, I yelped and had to walk out of there. I'm thinking, "No bullshit *this time,"* as though last time we were lying to you. Oscar heard me laugh, and he couldn't keep a straight face. "No bullshit this time."

And it was ridiculous, because that's supposed to be Billy's decision. What's Bergesch going to do about it anyway? He can't tell Billy who to play.

Oscar is living in a hotel right now with his wife and

daughter over in Rochelle Park. He's been telling Mumphrey, "Don't let them platoon you, Mumph. You better go ask to be traded." I found out that Oscar likes Mumphrey's house and wants to move in if Mumphrey gets traded. "Yeah, Mumph, you're right. They're not treating you right. You better go tell them you want to be traded."

Somebody asked Oscar, "How much longer are you going to live in that hotel?" Oscar said, "Right up until the time Mumphrey gets traded."

Oscar is in a strange situation where he's getting some of his money from San Diego. He played a spectacular season with Chicago, and at the end of it, he said he wanted a million and a half dollars. Ray Kroc got involved and said, "I'm going to give you ten minutes to accept this. I'm offering you three million dollars. Take it or leave it." Oscar was sputtering, "Where's the pen? Where do I sign?" The guys on the Padres called him Jesse James. Every time we run into an ex-Padre like Gene Tenace, he says to Oscar, "Hey, Jesse, how you doing?" Oscar goes, "Shush, be quiet. They don't call me that here."

I haven't been real happy, because it looks like Billy is going to start platooning me. Out in California he sat me against a tough left-hander, and then he did it in Oakland on a day game after a night game. But against Tommy John there was no reason to do it, other than it looks like I'm going to be platooned with Smalley at third.

Don Zimmer talked to me in Anaheim and said I was going to be playing against all right-handed pitching. He said that they have to have Robertson playing shortstop as often as they can. It looks like Smalley and I are going to be platooned at third base. That doesn't make me real happy. Campaneris will back up at second base and shortstop. It was kind of funny, because the night Zim said, "We want to have the kid in as much as we can," I looked at the lineup card, and Campaneris was playing third. I thought to myself, "Is that who he meant by the kid?" Campy is two years older than I am. They realize we can't win with Smalley at short every day, that they need Robertson. If he's going to develop as a player, they've got to start playing him now.

I guess they have to find someplace to play Smalley, and they figure if he doesn't have any range at short, he can play third. But it remains to be seen whether he even has the range to play third. I haven't really talked to Billy about it. When Zim told me that, he said, "Billy wants me to talk to you, and he'll talk to you also." But Billy never said anything about it. Billy has a way of delegating authority to his coaches to do a lot of his so-called dirty work. Maybe he doesn't feel he can talk to me about it. If it lasts much longer, I'm going to have to go and talk to him about it.

Also, in the back of my mind is some feeling that this is George's doing. I know Billy wants his best defense out on the field at all times, and we're better defensively with me at third and Robertson at short. Billy thinks that too. Maybe George finally got to him. I don't know. On this team you never know.

The pitchers say they'd rather have me at third. I hear their comments. They aren't real happy with Smalley's defensive play. But we're winning enough right now, so there is no way I want to create waves.

I've had eight hits in my last four games, which is pretty satisfying. I kept saying, "If Billy keeps me in the lineup, my luck is going to change." And it did change. I got a lot of satisfaction out of a three-run home run that beat Oakland. It was a big hit in a game when we weren't scoring any runs. It won the game for us, so it's been my most satisfying moment of the season. Mike Norris had struck me out the two times previously with fastballs, so he tried it a third time and he didn't get it in like he wanted to, and I hit it out.

We had had a meeting before the game, and we were chewed out by Billy for losing three straight in Anaheim. But it was clear that it was coming from George. We were reminded of the bottom line. It's always one bottom line or another. This time the bottom line was that attendance was down a hundred thousand. All they got to do is stick their heads out the door to realize it's been thirty or forty degrees out and raining every day this spring. If our record had been fifty and ten, I don't think we would have drawn any better. Nobody wants to come out to the park and freeze. That's why the attendance is down, not 'cause we've been playing bad.

My folks drove from San Diego to New York to see a game, and the weather got so bad they left halfway through. To say the attendance is down because we're not running away with the pennant, that's a bunch of bull. Plus school's not out yet.

We were told that if we didn't start winning, things were going to tighten up, that we were going to have to move out of some of the nicer hotels. We were going to start flying commercial instead of charter. George was going to spank our little butts if we didn't start producing for him. He's going to punish us. But that's how George operates. He likes to put fear in his employees' hearts. I can just see the headlines, "George Rooms Yankees in Cleveland YMCA as Punishment for Losing."

The rest of the meeting was pure Billy. It was a "stop making excuses" meeting, and I think guys were making excuses: the weather, the helter skelter lineups. Certain guys were complaining. Billy wanted them to stop complaining and start doing the job. I guess you can complain if you're doing the job. And yet if you're not playing, it's hard to do the job. This is going to be a sore point that will remain throughout the season.

The guys weren't too happy about the meeting. But you come to expect that sort of thing when you're playing for George.

One reason I would hate to have to platoon is that your emotions take such a beating. If you're a spot player, your emotions go way up and down, because you know if you go oh for four tonight, you might not play for three or four more nights. Then each at bat is such a trying experience. But if you know you're going to be in there every day, you don't worry that much. It's the same reason I'm glad I'm an everyday player and not a pitcher. If a pitcher takes a beating, he has to wait and think about it for three or four days. And if he's going real bad, maybe another two weeks before he gets in there. At least as a regular you can get right back in there the next day, get that bad game out of your mind.

Of course, the biggest reason I don't want to be a platoon player is that my contract expires at the end of the year, and then I am to become a free agent. George told my agent and me this winter that he would not negotiate during the season, and I don't want the other people around the league thinking, "If the Yankees are platooning Nettles, he mustn't be hitting well against left-handed pitchers." Especially when I'm hitting the lefties better than the righties. Maybe if I was on the first year of a five-year contract I could accept it, but right now I'm fighting for my baseball life, and I don't want anything to keep me from continuing my career. Also, I want us to win. First and foremost, it's a team game, and if I thought that this was the best way for us to win, I wouldn't say anything. I know Smalley has a productive bat and they've got to get him into the lineup somewhere, and I also know that Robertson is the best shortstop. I also know that the player who should be playing third base every day is me.

I have been hitting the ball outstandingly, but it's getting to be a joke, because during the entire road trip in the West I ended up with exactly two hits. I was hitting the ball hard three times a game. Guys were diving for balls who never dove for balls in their lives. It was as if every time I hit I was going to make a star out of somebody. I told my wife the other day, "They're getting back at me for all the times I've robbed them of hits through my career. It's starting to even up a little bit."

A kid from Texas named Tolleson took two or three hits away from me, dove up the middle for one ball, went into the hole the next time for another. First basemen are diving, catching the ball; the right fielder from Kansas City jumped up high on the fence to catch one. If I had any kind of luck, which I never had at the beginning of the year, I could be hitting .350. That's why I'm glad I have a manager who will stick with me and let me play myself out of my unlucky streak. It isn't a slump, because I'm hitting the ball well. Billy knows what's going on. He'll tell me, "You're swinging the hell out of the bat. Stay with 'em." That's all you can ask for in a manager. And the last five games I've been hitting the ball the same, but they've been finding holes, or going out.

Billy's being here makes such a tremendous difference. I know he's not going to let someone dictate to him what the lineup is.

I thought they were trying to do it to me a couple years ago when Howser was the manager. And I like Dick Howser. I like him a lot. Early in the year I was struggling, wasn't getting my hits, and so he pinch hit for me a couple of times. He even pinch hit a couple of rookies. One was Dennis Werth and one was Bobby Brown. These were guys who hadn't even been in the big leagues. That upset me even more. If I'm struggling, and they put in a guy like Piniella, fine. I can accept that.

I thought Howser, who had always touted the younger kids, was trying to make himself look good, hoping these kids would get hits so he could say, "Our young players are coming through.'' I broke a few lights in the runway, which was uncharacteristic. And I got out of the ballpark before the game was over, so there would be no confrontation with the press or with Howser. I felt I was being sacrificed so he could get his younger players in there. And I don't know why Dick did that. Unless he was under orders. But I know that would never happen with Billy.

There is nothing to replace intelligent defense. More than any other aspect of this game, intelligent defense is something that never shows up in the box score. The other players on the team understand and appreciate what it means to the team, but to really understand that, you have to play the game. That's why the writers don't understand it. I'm making the plays like I've always done, but the *Post* won't give me a break.

We were playing Oakland, and their right fielder, Mike Davis, tried to steal third. He overslid the base, rolling past it. At the same time the batter hit a fly ball to center field. Davis jumped back up and ran back to second to try to keep from getting doubled up.

Now I'm not saying this to blow my own horn, but merely to explain how intelligent defense can win you a ballgame. As he was stealing third, I saw both that he had a good jump and that the ball was hit in the air out toward center field. When I went over to cover third, I faked like there was a throw coming from the catcher. I knew that the Oakland players run with their heads down, without looking back at the hitter, so they are very easy to decoy, so I gave him the decoy, and he slid into the base and ended up over in foul territory, and I saw their coach, Clete Boyer, grab Davis and yell, "Get back to second." If the umpire had seen Clete touch the runner, he should have called him out right away. But he didn't call that.

But what I knew the umpire did see was that he didn't retouch third base going back to second. As the ball was being thrown in, and he was running back to second, I said to the umpire, "I hope you saw him not touch third base." And the umpire can't say a thing to me, but I could tell by the stony look he gave me that he saw he hadn't touched third. So when I did call for the ball and touched third, he called him out, and there was no argument from Oakland. It was late in a one to nothing game, and it kept them from scoring.

When we played Oakland back in New York, Willie Randolph, who has been the best second baseman in the league for years, suggested a play that won us a game. They had men on first and second, with Henderson the runner on second, and we made a pitching change. Randolph came to the mound and said to Wynegar, "If they're going to pull a double steal, there's no way to throw Henderson out at third. Let's throw it through to second base." Henderson got a great jump and stole third, and Butch threw to Willie at second and got the runner coming in by seven or eight feet. That's the only way to defense against that. That was good heads-up play by Randolph for suggesting it to Wynegar. It saved us another game.

BALLS

We're starting to come from behind to win games. Against Oakland we were tied nothing to nothing and scored a run late in the game. Then we went into Anaheim, and we were losing by four runs to the Angels, and we came back late in the game to go ahead, and then we got screwed on an umpire's call: Rudy May had Fred Lynn struck out, and the ump didn't call it a strike. He threw a beautiful curveball, and Lynn started to take a step toward the dugout, and the ump said ball three. May walked him, and he hit the next guy, and the next guy hit a ball that Oscar lost in the lights, and they got another bloop, and we ended up losing the game. But as far as we were concerned, that was a come-from-behind win. It showed us we can do it. In our minds we won that game.

We came from behind again against the Angels. Willie Randolph said to me after the game, "This is just like old times." That's what we used to do when we had the good teams. We'd go into the seventh inning, and we'd say, "Okay, this is our part of the game," and it wasn't just a cliché. We really meant it. We used to kill teams from the seventh inning on. Last year we didn't do it much at all, and earlier in the year we hadn't been doing it. In the last week we started doing it, and it's been reminding us of old times.

Goose has been part of our resurgence. When he's going good, you know if you have a three to two lead and he comes in, you're going to win it three to two. Earlier this year it wasn't that way because he was struggling, but he's back on beam, and that's a great feeling, because with him on, the team is starting to roll. We won six games in a row and are only a game and a half out, despite the turmoil.

1975–1976

eorge was under suspension in 1975 for making illegal campaign contributions to Richard Nixon, but that didn't stop him from running things. We knew Tricky George was behind everything that was going on. He just wasn't showing up at the ballpark to do them, which was probably fine with him, because we were playing that year at Shea, and not too many of us wanted to show up at Shea either.

The best thing George did that year was to acquire Catfish Hunter. As soon as a judge ruled that Oakland had breached Cat's contract and that he was a free agent, George went after him hard, offered him an astounding contract worth millions of dollars, and landed him. And I loved that.

Catfish was the first of the free agents, even though he had been freed on a technicality. But when George signed Catfish, we could see that George wasn't going to let any player pass by who could help us. In Cleveland or in Minnesota, they wouldn't have even made a bid on him. George could see that we needed a pitcher like Catfish, and he went out and got him. I was always impressed with the way George would go out and get the quality player, with money no object.

The other star the Yankees acquired that year was Bobby Bonds. George and Gabe traded Bobby Murcer to the Giants to get him. At the end of the '74 season George had told Murcer that he would be a Yankee as long as he owned the team. A month later, Bobby was traded to San Francisco, which is about as far from New York as you can ship a guy. I couldn't believe George could say that to a player and then trade him. But now that I know a little more about George, it's consistent. He says things and doesn't always keep his word. Why say them? That's what I don't understand. Maybe he was at a loss for words and just didn't know what else to say to Bobby at the time. After the season, though, Bobby was gone.

Afterward, George tried to say that Gabe had done it and not he. But nothing goes on without George's okay.

Bonds, who was supposed to be the big Yankee hero for years to come, was gone one year later. It was the story of his career. He would stay a year or two, and then he would be gone. He had good value, because he was a productive player. When someone needed a power hitter, they would ask for Bonds. But he struck out a lot, so he could never hit in the middle of the lineup because he would kill too many rallies. He was an ideal leadoff hitter. He would either strike out, homer, or start a rally. I played against him in the minor leagues, and he could do everything, run, hit, throw, hit for average, hit for power. But he struck out a lot. They make a big deal about the thirty-

thirty club, thirty homers and thirty stolen bases in one season. Bobby Bonds did it five times.

The one year Bonds was with us, he led the club in home runs, played when he was hurt, which was impressive, and was a good outfielder. He didn't cause any problems. He was great to have in the dugout and in the clubhouse. But he never was able to stay in one place too long, and it was no different with the Yankees. I don't know why so many teams were so ready to give him up in a trade. Gabe traded him to California for Mickey Rivers and Ed Figueroa.

The day after Gabe traded Murcer for Bonds, he sent Doc Medich to Pittsburgh and got Dock Ellis, Ken Brett, and Willie Randolph. Then Gabe traded Brett for Carlos May. Some good trades.

At the time we nicknamed Gabe Paul Monty Hall, after the emcee from *Let's Make a Deal*. A lot of it had to do with salaries. His overriding philosophy was to trade a big salary away for a smaller salary. That was foremost in his mind, even before talent. Bonds and Medich had far bigger salaries than the guys we got for them. His number-one priority is how much money he can save. Which makes those deals even more remarkable. He built the nucleus of our pennant-winning New York teams saving money all the way.

The one drawback to all that trading was that the rest of the players were looking around, asking themselves, "Who's going to be next?" Anytime you're on a team that Gabe Paul is running, you don't know where you stand from one moment to the next, because you know that as soon as you get your value up where your salary is going to go up, you're going to get traded. He won't keep players who he has to pay money to. And you know if you stay around you're never going to get a big salary, unless someone can overrule him, which George did. Of course with George, you never know whether you're going to stay around either. But unlike Gabe, he won't get rid of you just because you're making a lot of money. And it may well be one of the reasons Gabe moved on, because he was uncomfortable paying the big salaries George authorized.

We thought we had a good chance to win in '75. Our manager, Bill Virdon, did a good job in '74, even though everyone knew that his orders were coming directly from George. And even though we were having another good year in '75, George fired him. Virdon, a quiet man, wasn't box office.

We were only a few games out of first place. Billy had just been fired by Texas, and here was the first name-manager George could hire, and so he got him. George wanted Billy badly and got him even though Gabe Paul was dead set against it.

All of a sudden, one day we came to the park and Virdon was gone, and Billy was there. I loved the move, because I knew Billy from when I played for him at Denver and Minnesota. Some of the other guys, however, weren't so sure.

The next year, 1976, was a great deal of fun. It was the year I enjoyed most as a Yankee. We were returning to the stadium, and it was like, "We're home again, finally." The fans, our fans, were cheering us, and we had a great year. That was the year that Chris Chambliss homered against Mark Littell to beat Kansas City for the pennant.

George returned from exile in 1976, and it was Billy's first full year as manager. We got off to a real quick start, we were ahead the whole way, and for the most part George was pretty quiet.

The one big to-do came in August when George invited Dick Williams to sit with him in his private box. As I said earlier, George had tried to hire Williams the year before from Oakland, but Charley Finley refused to let him go unless the Yankees traded him two top prospects, which the Yankees wouldn't do. So we knew that George wanted Williams as manager.

We were sitting in the dugout before a game at the stadium, and we could see Dick Williams sitting in the box with George. That didn't set too well with Billy. He felt somebody was waiting in the wings to take his job, despite his having done a really good job that year. That was the first salvo in the battle between Billy and George. If I had been the manager, and George had done that to me, I would have been furious. And knowing George, George sat up there and second-guessed every move Billy made on the field. It had to unsettle Billy just for him to see Williams looking down on him like that. In reality, I don't think there was any significance in Williams' sitting up there. Here was a guy out of a job, and he was a friend of George's, and George invited him to watch the game. And yet, who knows? Just the fact that Williams was out of a job put pressure on all the other managers, including Billy. And Billy wasn't the most secure person in the world, not after having been fired at Minnesota, Detroit, and Texas.

After all the changes in managers I've seen George make all these years, maybe it *was* in George's mind to replace Billy with Williams. Billy and George had had some problems. Billy had screamed at George to get out of the clubhouse during spring training. And George is enamored of big names. Williams had won several pennants with Oakland, and he'd won at Boston. Yet I don't think George would have had an easier time with Williams, because Dick Williams is the same type of manager.

We won the pennant in '76. Billy had set up an exciting running game with Mickey Rivers, Roy White, and Randolph bunting, hitting-and-running, and stealing bases, and Chris Chambliss, Thurman, Oscar, and I were the big hitters. It was fun baseball. We ran away with the division, and I had more fun playing baseball than any time before or since, including '78. We had a set lineup, everyone knew exactly what his role was, Billy was clearly in charge, and everything clicked like it was supposed to, and there were no roadblocks or distractions. The players did their jobs, the manager did his job, the front office did its job, and everything went very smoothly. When you're winning right from the start, that alleviates a lot of potential problems. There didn't seem to be any problems that year.

We were back in the stadium, we had our fans back, and they were behind us all the way. We had been orphans playing at Shea, and now we were home, and people were coming out in droves, and we were playing well. We had a lot of laughs and the players were very close. We had a clique of Piniella, Munson, Catfish, Rivers, Randolph, Fred Stanley, Oscar Gamble, Carlos May, and myself, and Billy got along great with everybody. Often we would go out as a group. We would banter on the bus or on the planes. And we don't do that anymore. George got rid of almost every one of them and brought in much more serious people. The mood is different. In those days the players weren't nearly so sensitive to criticism. And much of it has to do with the big money they're now making. It's made everyone more serious.

In '76 I had a good year personally. I led the league in home runs. During the summer I had just gotten a new contract, which I thought was a good one. I was very happy. I could see myself as a Yankee for at least another couple of years, which in the Yankee organization is a long time. And by the end of the contract I was assured of becoming a ten and five player, so it gave me some security and made things easier.

Fans should understand that what's important to the players is not winning the World Series, but getting into it. In the American League playoffs in '76 we went the full five games against Kansas City, and we won the fifth game in the bottom of the ninth when Chris Chambliss homered against Mark Littell. We were at such an emotional peak that the World Series was almost a letdown.

It was funny. We came into the dugout the bottom of the ninth, and I told Carlos May, "Get ready to pick up all the gloves off the dugout. When someone hits a home run this inning, all the fans are going to come streaming in.'' No sooner did I say that than Chambliss hit the home run. Even before he crossed home plate, fans were flying onto the field.

It was the highest I ever felt on a baseball field. It was such a thrill to be part of history like that. We had been ahead, and then George Brett hit a three-run home run off Grant Jackson in the eighth to tie it up. At that point, we could have gone flat, but we came right back. Chambliss hit the home run and made a hero out of himself. A solo shot, bottom of the ninth. That's all we needed.

There was a picture of Chambliss hitting the ball and starting toward first base, which showed Thurman in the on-deck circle and Sandy Alomar coming out of the dugout with a bat jumping up and down. Someone wanted to use the picture for the next year's press guide, and George said, ''Cut Alomar out of that picture, because we're going to trade him.'' So they cut him out of the picture. You have to find the original picture to find Alomar.

It's very hard to reproduce in words what it felt like when Chambliss hit it out. We walked around the clubhouse slapping one another on the back and hugging one another for about a half hour after the game. It was very emotional. The clubhouse was filled with people. Everyone had his parents in, families. And then we celebrated hard that night. We had a party over at the Hasbrouck Heights Sheraton. We were all there until five in the morning. Then we had to catch an early bus to go to the airport and fly to Cincinnati. We weren't in any shape to play the World Series.

When we arrived in Cincinnati, we were still a little hung over from the celebrating we did after Chambliss's home run. That was Thursday, and we had to play the first game of the Series on Saturday afternoon. We only had a day and a half to recover, and we had celebrated hard.

We were also exhausted from running around trying to get World Series tickets for our families and friends. George took charge of the tickets to make sure all his Ohio cronies got theirs, and he absolutely refused to give us ours. He made us wait until five minutes before game time. Here we were, five minutes before the national anthem of the first game in Cincinnati, and we're running around, still trying to find someone to give us our tickets. There was a lot of screaming and yelling. Everyone was upset. Thurman was furious. It was like George was telling us that he got us to the Series all by himself and screw the players.

Five minutes before the national anthem, we got the tickets. It was bad enough that he stuck us in a hotel about an hour out of town, and we had to ride an old army bus, everybody cramped up, to play in the World Series. And I don't know whose fault that was, but I never could understand why they did that to us after what we did for them.

The fans might not think that the ticket mess is a particularly big deal, but it is. You're in your first World Series, and you want to make sure your wife at least has a seat. We never did get our feet on the ground, and by the time we got settled, we had lost in four straight. They just blew us away.

We played a Sunday night game, and it was about twenty-five degrees. Our commissioner, Buffoon Bowie, was sitting over in his box in his shirtsleeves. We noticed him all right. He was either trying to show how tough he was—actually he was just showing how stupid he was—or he was pretending to the world it wasn't cold, but as a player I can tell you it was too cold to be playing baseball that night.

Afterward Cincinnati manager Sparky Anderson added insult to injury. Thurman Munson hit about .570 in the Series, and we went into the press room after the final game, and someone asked Anderson, "What did you think of Thurman?" He said, "Don't ever try to compare him with Johnny Bench." Thurman was sitting right there at the table, and it embarrassed the hell out of him. It showed a lack of class on Anderson's part. Bench may have been Series MVP, but Anderson could have been more tactful. Thurman was an unusually sensitive person, and he really put Thurman down in front of everybody. Thurman never did forget that.

George didn't either. He was furious we had lost four straight, told everyone how embarrassed he was, as he often does. He swore it wouldn't happen again. The next year, when it came time for the first free agent draft, he made his move. He signed Don Gullett and Reggie Jackson. The days of quiet dignity were over.

7

Rudy May is on Billy's bad side. When they tried to trade him to the White Sox over the winter, Rudy said, "I'm glad I'm here, because I don't like Billy Martin that much," and the next day they found out there was something wrong with the deal, that he couldn't be traded to the White Sox. After Rudy's burned his bridges behind him, he's back with the ballclub. It didn't set too well with Billy. And when Rudy pitches, he has incredibly bad luck. Three games in a row he's thrown strike three to get us out of an inning, and the umpire hasn't called it, and the next pitch the guy's gotten a base hit or a home run. It happened out in Anaheim, and in Milwaukee he had a guy struck out, the umpire calls ball three, and a couple pitches later, boom, a base hit, and we lost the game.

After the game he was in a good enough mood, but on the plane Rudy threw a tantrum. He was sitting in the back next to me with a seat between us. He was punching at the window. I finally said, "Rudy, knock it off. You're 'not going to help things doing that. You're just going to hurt yourself or hurt the plane.''

He stopped, but then he threw his food tray up in the air and started kicking and screaming and stomped off into the bathroom. He and Goose started yelling at each other. Goose was trying to quiet him. Goose said, ''Grow up. You're not the only guy who ever lost a game.'' The airplane crew got upset because of the commotion. Billy had to come back and calm Rudy down. And then about ten days ago, while he was home packing for a road trip, his back blew out on him. The guys went up to pick him up in the morning, and they found Rudy lying on the floor in pain screaming, and they had to call an ambulance and put him in the hospital. I haven't talked to Rudy since. He's been in the hospital in traction. That's a strange one. It could be a major injury. I'm glad for Rudy that he got a two-year contract out of the ballclub last year. If this had happened in the last year of his contract, at his age the wrong people might tend to forget about him.

There are always rumors as the trading deadline approaches. We thought for sure Mumphrey was going to be traded. He wanted to be traded, and we had too many outfielders, so it only figured he would go. But he didn't. And I was surprised we only made the one trade for Matt

Keough. To get him we gave up one of our best minor league pitchers, a kid named Callahan. The other minor leaguer in the deal was Marshall Brandt, who was like Balboni. Brandt hit thirty home runs every year in Triple-A, and the Yankees didn't seem to want him in the major leagues. He got in and helped Oakland win a game last night. Callahan pitched and won a game for the A's. I'm glad to see these guys producing now that they've gotten a chance to play in the big leagues. There are many times when the Yankees tell you, "We're doing this for your own good." Yeah, sure. Front office people have a way of trying to make you believe what they want you to believe. They think they're dealing with twelve-year-olds rather than grown men.

I was sure we were going to get a right-handed pitcher. In fact, a couple days before the trading deadline, Art Fowler asked me, "Who would you rather have, Jim Beattie or Matt Keough?" They were both being shopped around. I thought about it for a minute and I said, "We would probably be better off with Keough, because Beattie has been here once before, and maybe he wouldn't be happy pitching in this atmosphere." Not that he's not a good pitcher. But he didn't seem to do well here last time—George had humiliated him publicly, sent him down to the minors when he didn't pitch well. Keough might not be intimidated right from the start like Beattie might be. Whether my opinion had any effect on the deal, I don't know, but we ended up getting Keough for a couple of minor leaguers, so I thought it was a good deal for us. Billy started him in Baltimore, and he pitched real well. I expected more trading to be done, because with all the talk about how the club was having so much trouble winning, I thought there would be a big shakeup. But there wasn't. And they surprised me when they kept Mumphrey. I thought Mumph had a lot of trading value, and if we did need pitching, he would be the one we could get a top pitcher for. Unless his salary is so high no one wanted him. That's what George said about all of us at the beginning of the year. I just thought that trading Mumphrey for a starting pitcher would have been one way to relieve a problem.

Billy and George are having a go-around. After a home stand during which we blew a couple games in the late innings, we flew off for Milwaukee. We were scheduled for an off day, but George wanted us to have a workout. It was the first day of the road trip, we hadn't had a day off in almost a month, and Billy didn't want it. He doesn't believe in using workouts to punish his players the way George does. Billy made it voluntary and ten or eleven guys showed up. George didn't like that.

What is happening is that even though this is the third time around for Billy and George, George is trying to test Billy, to see if he can push Billy around.

While we were still at home, we were told we would be leaving on the off day at five o'clock. And then the day before we left, we were handed itineraries that said we were leaving at eleven in the morning. This was so we could have the workout in Milwaukee. It wasn't Billy's itinerary. It was sent from the front office, and it really upset Billy. He told the guys, "I don't believe you need a workout. You need a day off more," and he was right. All it did was foul up our sleeping habits for a couple days. We had just played a night game, and instead of being able to sleep in the next morning and leave at five in the afternoon, we had to get up at eight in the morning and catch an early flight. It fouled us up for the entire Milwaukee series, though George would never admit that that was the reason we didn't play well. But that was it. We were in a daze the first couple days.

After the Milwaukee series, we moved on to Cleveland, where we lost a couple more games. George was there, and it didn't look good for Billy. George was still furious that so many of us missed the workout. We heard that Billy was going to be fired right on the spot. The Cleveland papers had Billy fired. What George did instead was fire Art Fowler, knowing that he and Billy were so close. George had been making a lot of noise about shaking up the team, getting rid of the manager, getting new players, and I think he finally said to himself, "I better do something." He couldn't fire Billy. He had just hired him for a third time and given him a million-dollar contract. So he figured he would do the next best thing to get to Billy. He fired Art, to force Billy into quitting and in that way get out of the big contract Billy had.

Billy called me aside in Cleveland, and he said, "I've been going around and around with George, and now we're going at it again."

He said, "Our first big argument was in the spring over you. He wanted to get rid of you, and I didn't, and that made him angry. Now he's insisting on having these workouts, and he wants to get rid of Art. He's trying to get me in a pissed-off mood so that I'll quit. But I'm not going to let him force me into quitting. I'm not happy about his firing Art, but there isn't much I can do about it right now."

I sat there and listened. Billy needs someone he can trust to talk to. I feel fine, as captain of the team and as his friend, that he can come to me any time to confide in me. Sometimes he tells me what's on his mind, because we've been together for so long. He'll ask my opinion on certain things, not that I'm trying to counsel him, but I'll try to calm him down if I see a confrontation coming, because he's awfully stubborn and George is awfully stubborn, and it might take a third party's opinion to keep them from locking horns. Any time I can help Billy out, I'll give him my piece of advice.

I said, "I don't blame you for being pissed off, Billy. I'd feel the same way if they fired one of my coaches. Try not to let the man get to you. Try to put all this bullshit out of your mind when you get out there on the field." I can see it wearing on Billy. Billy wants to concentrate on the game, and he has all these other distractions, and it makes it tough for him.

We lost two games to Cleveland, and we dropped a little in the standings, and then the stories started about how George was upset with Billy's conduct, how Billy supposedly had sloppy work habits, and he was accused of talking to a woman sitting next to the dugout in

Milwaukee. When I'm on the field, I always glance into the dugout between pitches to see whether Billy wants anything done on the field. I never saw him with his back turned talking to anybody in the stands. A reporter wrote it in the paper, and then George accused him of it. But I didn't see it. People are sticking their heads in the dugout all the time, or yelling things, or asking for autographs. You say something to them, try to be polite to them, or tell them to get the hell out. I never saw Billy with his head turned toward the stands during the game as he was accused of doing.

George also accused him of taking a nap during batting practice. That's not a terrible thing in itself. But I don't think Billy was taking naps. I think it was his way of getting away from the press. He gets hounded a lot, so he closed the door for an hour and told the clubhouse man to tell the press he was taking a nap, when in reality he was sitting in there and watching TV. And even if he was napping, it's not material. There's nothing wrong with that.

One night in Cleveland Billy called me into his office. He said, "You know what I did? I went home after the game, locked the door, locked myself in my room. I was in such a pissed-off mood, if I had gone out and had a couple drinks, there's no telling what might have happened."

That was the day he smashed the urinal in the dugout with a chair. I didn't even know about that until after the game. It must have happened while we were out in the field. Cleveland scored six runs in the first inning, and I guess he was upset, and he went down and tore up the urinal. And George was on his ass for that. I'm not saying players do it all the time, but players have been known to break urinals, or lights in the runway. It's a long runway from the dugout to the clubhouse in Cleveland, and after the game I walked by the urinal and saw that it was all busted up and that all the light bulbs were smashed in the runway. After the game Piniella said, "I'm going to go out there tomorrow with a flashlight taped to my helmet so I can get back up to the clubhouse after the game." Walking down that runway with no lights is like walking down a mine shaft.

After the two losses to Cleveland, George was saying that the players had shamed themselves. Any time we lose to Cleveland in Cleveland, he's furious. George wants everyone to think he's from New York, but he isn't; he's from Cleveland. So he takes losses in Cleveland harder than he takes other losses, 'cause he has so many friends there. Or people who know him, let's put it that way. I don't know if they're actually his friends.

We didn't shame ourselves. It was just a couple of old-fashioned ass-kickings we got. Any major league team can beat the hell out of any other major league team. Not just beat them, but beat the hell out of them. And Cleveland did, they beat us badly, and we had no excuses.

George's problem is that he wants to win the pennant by July. He wants to be ten games out in front by the end of May. It can't work that way in our division. It's a slow process, and if we're going to win, we're going to do it in August and September, not in May and June like he wants to. He's such an anxious guy. We can win ten games in a row, and then if we lose two, he'll say we shamed ourselves. He can't believe that a team with an inferior salary can beat a team with such a high salary. Everything is dollars and cents to him, and he can't understand how a rookie making a minimum salary can strike out Dave Winfield who's making millions. It's beyond him, because he's never played the game. He'll never be able to figure that one out.

There were some strange goings on for about a week. The day after Henry Hecht wrote an article saying, "Art Fowler doesn't know anything about pitching," George got rid of Fowler. Henry must have known beforehand from George that George was going to get rid of him. Why shouldn't that backstabbing dwarf do George's dirty work for him? Do you think George knew that "scrounge" Henry would gladly shove it to Billy?

When George fired Art, Ron Guidry said that he was going to dedicate the season to Fowler. Gid said that Fowler was the best pitching coach he ever had. Whose word are you going to take as far as whether Art is a good pitching coach, Henry Hecht's or Ron Guidry's? Henry loses all his credibility right there. He doesn't have much credibility in the first place. Unfortunately, that doesn't do Art, or Billy, much good. In Yankee society, Ron Guidry is no match for the one-two punch of George and Henry Hecht.

The day they fired Art, Billy came to the ballpark in a sour mood. You can't blame him. They had just gotten rid of his best friend. He came into the clubhouse about four o'clock, and there was this lady there. Billy said, "What the hell are you doing in here? Who are you?" She said, "I'm conducting a survey, just like always." I didn't remember anyone ever conducting a survey. Billy said, "Get on out of here. We don't do that stuff at this time." She said, "I'm from the *New York Times.*" Billy said, "I don't care who you're from. Get your ass out of the clubhouse." And when she wouldn't move, he said, "I told you to get your ass and your survey out of this clubhouse." She said, "But I'm from the *New York Times.*" He said, "You can tell the *New York Times* to Kiss my dago ass." And I was standing right there with four or five of the other players. I heard Billy say that word for word. And then we find out that the girl has complained to her editor that Billy had said, "Why don't you suck my dick?" And that was the furthest thing from the truth.

Afterward I started to read all these stories about how Billy had abused her. It was almost like he was being set up. Some of us players were wondering about it afterward. We immediately suspected George had sent her to provoke an incident so he could fire him. With the mood

114

Billy was in, why did this girl have to show up that day? It was as though someone wanted him to lose his cool so he could be fired. I thought he handled himself fine. He wasn't out of line at all. It's what he would have said to any male reporter. Billy was being accused unjustly that time. I know it for a fact.

We had never seen that girl reporter before, and we'll probably never see her again. It was funny. That day I walked into the stadium about fifty feet behind Oscar Gamble, and this girl came through the barricades and came up to Oscar and tried to get Oscar to get her into the clubhouse. Oscar said, "I can't do anything for you." I walked in right afterward, and she didn't say anything to me, because I slipped right by her. Twenty minutes later I saw her in the clubhouse. I immediately wondered to myself, "What's going on?" If she was official, why didn't the *New York Times* arrange for her credentials? Why was she bothering the players to get into the clubhouse? Something was very, very strange there.

After the incident with the *New York Times* girl, there was an article in the *Post* that said "several players hoped the Yankees would get a new manager. Billy has already lost his team, said one player." You have to take into consideration who writes these articles. If it's Henry Hecht, he never names a player. He'll just throw his own thoughts out and blame a player for it. If certain writers want to get a manager, they can go on quoting unnamed sources forever. I'm sure certain players would be happy with a different manager. Billy knows that. But I think the majority of the players would rather have Billy as the manager.

Mike Lupica in the *News* also wrote an article against Billy. Lupica said "we have a scared team in a chaotic situation," but from what I can see, that just isn't true. The only thing chaotic is that nobody knows from one day to the next whether he's going to be playing. And that certainly isn't Billy's fault. The players believe in Billy, and they do do what he says. Sometimes they don't like it, but they do respect him enough to do what he says. And that's not always the case on a veteran team.

There's no way we're a scared team, like Lupica says. There is nothing to be scared of. Most of us are veterans who have been around. I don't see anything to be scared of. I really have no idea what Lupica is talking about.

I don't know why the writers would want Billy fired. He helps them write their stories for the day. If they had a guy like Bob Lemon around, they'd have to work hard for their stories. With Billy around, there is always going to be a story. That's why the press was so upset when the Yankees got rid of Reggie. He was another guy who was always good for a story. Look at the *Post*. One day it had Dr. Joyce Brothers analyzing Billy. Billy has gotten the Yankees in the papers, and he's even taking them out of the sports section! Here are the Yankees in every part of the paper. What more could George possibly want from the guy?

I won the finale in Cleveland with a home run. The writers came up to me after the game and said, "How do you feel about being Billy's good friend and getting the big hit that probably saved his job?" I said, "I didn't know his job was on the line. I don't know what you're talking about." They said, "Didn't you see the article in the Cleveland paper saying that Billy was going to be fired?" I had been reading a novel called *Cinnamon Skin* by John McDonald, and I said real coldly, "If it's not in this book right here, I don't know nothing about it." And they kind of walked away from me. They thought they were going to get some great quote about how I had saved Billy's job.

That's always a question, whether his job is really on the line or whether George is playing around in the newspapers. I think it was a master plan to get the headlines, because two days later, on the fifteenth, the Mets made a big trade with St. Louis, getting Keith Hernandez, and in the New York papers George got the headlines, because he was about to fire Billy. Which is what he wanted. He wanted those headlines. And he took the Mets right off the front page.

For two weeks there were banner headlines about whether or not Billy was going to be fired. If it had been up to the *Daily News*, Billy would never manage in the majors again.

Dick Young of the *Post* accused the *Daily News* of trying to get Billy fired. Maybe we can get the papers fighting with each other. Things start and build and blow up like a tornado, and then all of a sudden everything is calm. After the incident with the *Times* researcher, everything quieted down.

The whole first half of the season has been like a boxing match, like two fighters trying to feel each other out. George is trying to find out whether Billy has changed since the last time he was here. He wants to see if he can push him around, if he can order him to do things. And I think he's discovered that Billy is still his own man, that he's not going to be able to dictate to him. And as long as we keep winning, things will remain calm the rest of the year.

To George this is nothing more than a huge Broadway play, and his job is to make money and to put people in the seats, and he feels if he can get our name in the paper every day, whether it be good or bad, it's going to get people talking about the Yankees. And it has. We've always had good attendance with Billy as manager. I just wish there was another way to go about it, because it puts a lot of pressure on the players, and a lot of pressure on the manager, and that's not the way to play baseball. You should play the game relaxed, not fearful. I say again, George, never having played the game, doesn't realize that. He wants to put fear into everybody like he does into the people who build his boats. When we're out on the field, there's always somebody standing in front of a line drive or a ground ball, somebody trying to prevent your hitting the ball. But when there's someone on the assembly line making a boat, there's no one standing over him, trying to knock the hammer out of his hand. He has to be able to separate the two. George will never learn that you cannot scare people into doing well in baseball.

From where I sit, the Yankees are doing extremely well. We're only three games out, hanging right in, despite some injuries. It's just that people like the owner and the writers don't realize that the reason we're in fourth place is that there are a couple other teams in front of us, Toronto and Detroit, who are normally second-division teams. If they had their normal start, then we would be four or five games better than we are now, and no one would be complaining. But there's tremendous parity in the American League East this year—Toronto is strong with their good young pitching, and Detroit has some new young talent—and that should stop any team from running away with it this year. It used to be that you had to win a hundred games to win the pennant. This year ninety should do it. Take Don Zimmer, our third-base coach. We get on Zim quite a bit about how during the late seventies when he was managing Boston, one year he won one hundred, another ninety-eight, and another ninety-seven, and he didn't win anything. The division used to have two or three strong teams, and the rest were lousy. Now there are six teams that are real strong.

Look at Toronto. Toronto has done the right thing. They started with a young team three years ago, and they didn't win, but they stuck with those guys, let them develop, and now they're starting to win. The only other team that did that was Oakland of the early seventies. They started together in the late sixties, and they were lousy at first. Yet Finley stuck with them. After five years together they became world-beaters.

Toronto's doing the same thing. They're keeping their young kids together and letting them mature as a team.

Plus they have great pitching. They're not a fluke. The guy who's doing it is Pat Gillick, who when he left the Yankees took a lot of our young players with him. He took Upshaw, Iorg, the third baseman, another guy. He started with young talent and stayed with them. Plus they have a good manager, Bobby Cox, who all the young kids can relate to. Before Bobby, they had a bunch of young kids and then hired a manager, Roy Hartsfield, who was almost seventy years old. And after that they had another guy older than him. Finally, they hired Cox, and he relates well to them, and they're doing much better. It remains to be seen whether they're going to be able to handle the pressure of a tight pennant race in September in front of forty thousand people, but they have enough pitching to carry them there.

The Orioles are right behind Toronto, even though Jim Palmer's been out the first two months of the season, and one of their top pitchers, Dennis Martinez, is four and ten. They haven't had Mike Flanagan for the last six weeks. And here they are right up there! It's amazing. Talk about manager of the year: I'd have to give it to Joe Altobelli. I can't imagine where we would be if Guidry or Shane were hurt and if Righetti were four and ten for the first two months. Joe has done an amazing job.

Baltimore is another stable organization that brings up certain key players, nurtures them, and keeps them. They work through their farm system, rather than signing three free agents every year. It isn't flamboyant, but they have proved that if you have intelligent people in the front office making decisions, you can field a superior team without having to shell out all that money. The Dodgers do it that way too.

It's got to be disheartening for the players in the Yankee farm system, knowing they can have good year after good year after good year and still there's no job for them. The minor leaguers in those other organizations know that they're going to be rewarded for their play by a trip to the big leagues. Bones Balboni is back at Columbus again. For his sake, I was wishing he would be traded, to get him out of this organization where he can play. I don't think they're going to give him much of a shot. They're always trying to say, "We're doing what's best for you"—that's the line they always give you. It's like "The check is in the mail." He's a kid who's twenty-five years old, and he's got to start playing in the big leagues. I wish they would give him to some other organization, because I don't think we're going to use him. He's a good kid. Maybe if he complained, popped off a little bit, they would do something with him. But he comes up here for three weeks, and you don't hear two words out of him the whole time.

Lou Piniella gets to play once a week and gets two or three hits every time he does. Lou has hitting down to a science. There are very few guys who worry about their swings as much as he does and are still able to produce. Smalley and Lou are inseparable. They're always standing in front of a mirror or working with each other trying to get the perfect swing. It's become a joke. When I see them, I say, "This is Leonard Nimoy along with Lou Piniella and Roy Smalley, in search of . . . the Perfect Swing." Roy White and I get a laugh out of it every time. They kind of mumble away at me.

Lou's got a new stance. He just started using it the other night. He says he's opened it up. Except that it looks just like his old one. I said, "Can we expect to see Smalley using that stance in the next couple of days?" He said, "No. No. This one is just for me." They work so hard on their swings. They look at films, they talk about their shoulders doing this and their hips doing that, and their toes doing this. When Lou goes up there he must have a hundred things running through his mind as the pitch is coming to the plate. Lou is always thinking: Where are my hands? Where is my stride? Where is my elbow? Where is my shoulder? Whereas I try not to think about anything at the plate. Some guys can experiment and change stances, but if I had to keep changing every game, I'd be a mess. Lou keeps saying that he is changing his stance, but every stance looks the same to me. He has 245 different stances, but they all look the same.

Smalley's having a good year offensively, but for all the work he's done on his hitting, he still looks the same as he did when he came to the ballpark last year. I don't know what minor technicalities they're working on, but you sure can't tell by looking at them with the naked eye. But among the players it's a joke. We watch them and giggle. "Oh, God, here they go again working on their swings."

Roy White was walking by the other day, and Lou

tossed him a bat and said, "Hold your bat this way. What do you think?" An hour later Roy was still standing there, holding up the bat. I asked Roy, "Have you joined the search party too? Have you joined up with Lou and Smalley and Leonard Nimoy?"

To give Lou his due, he has worked a lot with Andre Robertson to get Andre to stop swinging up on the ball. Andre swings at a lot of high pitches with an uppercut, so he hits nice high flies up in left center field. To be effective, Andre is going to have to use his speed, to hit the ball on the ground or on a line. And he has started doing that.

As far as I'm concerned, Andre is the best shortstop in the league right now. He covers more ground than any other. If he's still hitting after a couple more trips around the league, we'll know he's arrived.

Oscar plays about as infrequently as Lou does, and whenever he gets in, he produces. It takes a special talent to do that. I don't know if I could come off the bench once a week and play like Oscar and Lou do.

Oscar's got a bit of a gut on him. I told him, "Oscar, you look like you're always ready for a basketball game." He said, "What do you mean?" I said, "You got a basketball under your shirt." That Oscar, he's always jabbering on about something. He hardly ever shuts up.

A couple weeks ago we had a talk by the FBI and the drug enforcement people—they were talking to every club about drugs and gambling. This guy was telling us how you can get stuck by a drug dealer who can get you hooked, and then he'll have something on you, and he'll get you to throw a game. After the meeting, Oscar referred to it as a talk by ''Epplin Zepplin Junior.''

Bowie Kuhn came out and said he had spies out in the bars and restaurants the ballplayers hang out in, trying to catch people. On the day of George's infamous workout, Goose and I spent most of the day trying to find Bowie Kuhn's spies. We went to quite a few places around Milwaukee. Finally after about four hours, we decided the moose hanging on the wall of this one bar was a spy, because we had been in another bar that had a moose on the wall. Goose said, ''That's the second moose we've seen today.'' It was obvious: Bowie had sent a moose to spy on us.

The other shoe finally dropped on Bobby Murcer. It was a matter of time before Murcer went into the announcing booth. He was strictly a designated hitter. He refused to play in the outfield. Said he couldn't. So when

Griffey got hurt, we needed a first baseman—outfielder, and Don Mattingly was the ideal guy to call up from Columbus. Mattingly's going to be good. He does everything fundamentally well. He's hit everywhere he's been in the minor leagues. As much as I hate to say it, he's going to be of more value to the club than Murcer was. Bobby's a good friend and could have helped us if they had let him be the designated hitter every day. But as long as they weren't going to use him, then we're better off with Mattingly.

That same day Rene Lachmann was fired by Seattle. To me it's suicide to fire a manager in the middle of the season. It helps so much to have one manager. You get to know his thinking, and then you can play the way he wants you to play. The last couple years we've had an army of managers. By the time you finally adjust to the manager, learn his philosophy, his thinking, he gets fired. And you have to adjust to a new manager. Say what you want about Billy, when you know he's in your corner, it makes playing the game of baseball much easier. I just hope George will let him stay awhile.

Somebody'll jump on Lachmann quickly, because he's an excellent young manager. I've watched him against us, and he always makes the right moves. His problem was being stuck with a team that doesn't have very much talent. He's a fine manager. I'd like to play for him.

The same day Seattle fired Lachmann it got rid of Gaylord Perry and Todd Cruz. Cruz was one of the team leaders in RBIs and home runs, and even though he's only hitting two hundred, how many shortstops come along who can hit with power? Baltimore picked him up immediately, solving their third-base problem. As for Gaylord, I guess Seattle decided to go with their young pitchers. From what I read, Gaylord was critical of his teammates, which he always has been in the past. He gets on players who make errors behind him. When we were together on the Indians, I was aware of it, but he never said anything to me. I don't know what I would have done if he had. I know if he had gotten on me on the field, there might have been a scene. Fortunately, it never came up. You can't criticize teammates during a game. It doesn't sit too well.

I looked at the lineup card before a game against Milwaukee, didn't see my name, and walked into Billy's office to talk to him about it. George was there. I told Billy, "I think I should be in there against this guy." Billy put me in, and I went out and had a good game. It was against Rick Waits, who was pitching for Milwaukee at the time. It's one thing to tell Billy you should be in there, but with George hearing that, if I had gone out there and fallen on my face, George would have had every right to come down on Billy and say, "Why are you letting the players tell you when to play them?" But I got a double the first time up, hit the ball hard, and after the game, George told the writers I had confounded him.

George told the *Daily News,* "If Nettles' second half is as good as his first, I'll declare him the eighth wonder of the world right up there next to the Leaning Tower of Pisa."

George must have figured I was ready to fall down, or at least was leaning that way, I guess. George can never compliment anyone straight out. He can't say, "I'm completely satisfied. I think he's done great." He always has to qualify it. He has to say, "He's done well, but let's see how he does in the second half." If I have a good year this year he'll say, "If he can do it five more years, then I'll say he's a good player."

It was about as good a compliment as I could get out of a guy like George. But he did say that I had confounded him. I guess that means I fooled him, showed him to be wrong. I don't quite know why he compared me to the Leaning Tower of Pisa. I'm not even Italian. And not only is the Leaning Tower of Pisa not one of the wonders of the world, it's also bad architecture.

The only thing that's unsettling right now is Willie Randolph's injury. He was upset that he pulled his hamstring again in Boston. He rushed himself back into the lineup because he had been reading in the newspapers that he doesn't play injured, that he's not a gamer. It started getting to him, and he came back sooner than he should have, and he hurt himself even worse this time. It was sad. He keeps seeing things written about him. "So and so on such and such a team is playing with a torn-up knee or whatever, and here is Randolph still sitting on the bench with a bruise." Finally he just said, "Hell, put me back in the lineup." After a couple games, he hurt himself again.

With Willie hurt so often, we've needed extra infielders. We brought up Barry Evans. He's going to fill in where he's needed. Smalley'll play first, and now that Griffey has healed I imagine he'll play center. Occasionally Smalley'll play third to rest me against certain left-handers. I can't see me losing my job right now the way things are going.

I started the month hitting six home runs in the first twelve games. After I hit the first two or three, I could feel another hot streak coming on. I know I'm going to hit six or seven within a ten- to twelve-day period. It's been that way all through my career. I know it's going to be a hot streak, and I know it's going to end, and I just hope it doesn't for a while.

I hit a couple of home runs against Seattle, off Gaylord Perry, and another off Bill Caudill, and it just seemed I was hitting a home run every other day. Even when I wasn't hitting home runs, I was coming real close. Guys were jumping over the fence to catch them. In Cleveland, Gorman Thomas went over the fence and took a home run away from me in straightaway center field. Or I was hitting them right against the fence. Or else I'd hit the ball just foul. I get in a groove where I hit a lot of long fly balls. And that's when the home runs begin.

My numbers are respectable for this time of year. I care about the numbers only because other people are looking at them. I know we have so many quality players on this team that if your numbers aren't good, it gives them an excuse to put you on the bench. And I'm concerned about my numbers this year, because I know that if I don't produce, I won't stay in the lineup.

Andre has got to play shortstop for us to win. It was evident against Baltimore Monday night. Shane Rawley started, and we won in extra innings 4–3. But there were many balls hit over in the hole or over the bag at second, and Andre was all over the place. He made a name for himself that night on national television. He played well. I played well next to him. It was a shame we got rained out the next night. A win like that can give you momentum, but when you lose a day after a game like that, it gives the other team a day to forget about it and fight back. If we could have played and won Tuesday night, we could have been on a roll. An extra-inning win against Baltimore, a team in our own division that was in first place, was the most emotional game we played all year. The crowd was relatively small, about twenty-five thousand, but for the players and the people who came, it was a playoff atmosphere. And it was a good game.

I was surprised to be hitting second. I've had good success against Scotty McGregor. They got off to an early lead when Sakata hit a home run off Shane, and then Shane gave up more bloop hits. And then we fought back. We got a run at a time and kept within range, and we never got behind more than two runs. We tied it up in the ninth, which was great, and we went ahead and won it in the eleventh. Wynegar, who had gotten to the park late because he had been at a funeral in Minnesota for his father-in-law and then hit into two double plays, got the hit that won it. As soon as he got the hit, we ran out onto the field to congratulate him. I told him, "I knew you couldn't hit into another double play, because there were two outs when you got up." He laughed.

You could tell by how the guys reacted to the win that it was an important game.

Goose was pitching well, when we didn't even think he would be able to pitch. In Boston he tried to impress his wife and take her to a nice restaurant. He ordered lobster, and the lobster bit him back. He cracked open a claw, and one of the thorns on it went right into the fingernail on the index finger of his pitching hand. The next day I told him, "Goose, cheeseburgers don't bite back. What are you trying to do?" He said, "Puff, you're right. I was definitely out of my league. From now on it's back to cheeseburgers." The next day his finger was really bothering him, and the trainers had him stick the finger into a lime for most of Sunday to heal it. Goose said his finger was throbbing, but the trainers told him not to worry, that the lime would heal it faster than anything, and they were right. The next day he pitched three innings and looked like the Goose of old.

Goose hadn't had a save in weeks. It used to be that you would bring Goose in and you had the confidence that they weren't going to get a hit, never mind score a run. Lately, when he's come in, he's been giving up runs. He can't understand it. We can't understand it. He looks like he's throwing the same, but it seems that he hasn't been having any luck. Baltimore was the first game when he blew a team away. If he keeps on like that, it's going to be a fun race the rest of the year.

1976–1977

I was aware all through 1976 that Andy Messersmith was playing the season out unsigned. We all knew that. Dave McNally was doing the same thing, though he didn't play. He sat out, but he was still part of the legal battle. I don't think enough players understand what Messersmith went through. Every player ought to thank Andy Messersmith for all the money they're getting these days. He was the only one who had enough balls to do that. And it was over not much more than thirty thousand dollars, which is nothing compared to the numbers thrown around these days.

A couple other players like Sparky Lyle started that season without contracts, but they backed down before the season was over and signed. Andy is a very stubborn person. He went through with it. The Dodgers are supposed to be *the* organization, but they made some blunder with him. They told Andy, "Well go ahead, take us to arbitration." And as it got closer to arbitration, they realized they were going to lose the case, and they went back and offered him the thirty thousand they wouldn't give him before, and he said, "The hell with you. I've gone this far. I might as well just keep going with it."

It was a great day for the players when the mediator ruled that Andy was free, that the reserve clause no longer bound the players to their teams. And yet, I—and most of the players—had no idea what this was going to mean in terms of salary. We had no idea that George was going to go crazy and shell out the millions of dollars a year he's been shelling out, or that there would be other owners who would do the same thing.

Thus, even though I was aware of what Andy was doing, I decided to sign a three-year contract halfway through my option year in '76 calling for a salary of $120,000 the first year, with a nice raise in each of the next two years. I felt George was offering me a good deal.

As a result of the Messersmith arbitration decision, the first free agent draft was held during the winter of 1976. The Yankees picked Bobby Grich, Don Baylor, Gullett, Gary Matthews, Wayne Garland, Reggie, Campaneris, and a couple of lesser players.

And when I saw the contracts George offered the free agents it made my stomach upset. We were the guys who had made the Yankees an attractive team, the ones who had turned them into a winner, and he gives the new players all the money. Thurman had a verbal promise from George that he would always be the highest-paid Yankee, except for Catfish. George reneged on that within a matter of months. When Reggie came over, Thurman waited for George to raise his salary like he had promised. When he didn't, Thurman was furious for a long, long time.

I didn't think anyone would offer contracts that big. It

just shows that there has always been a lot of money to be made in baseball and that before, the owners were making it all.

I got squeezed in the middle, but I'm not complaining. Sometimes you take a gamble, and you can't complain if you bet wrong. I wasn't prepared to go to free agency. It was the first year. I didn't know how the other clubs were going to react. I didn't realize the owners were as greedy as they were. In the last seven or eight years they have proved that they aren't afraid to stab one another in the back.

At the time I didn't understand how George could give Reggie all that money, something like $2.8 million, what with Reggie being such a liability in the field. He gave him the highest salary in all of baseball at the time. Where I had worked awfully hard on my defense and had become a very good third baseman as well as hitting with power, here was someone else getting five times more money for being just a one-way player. It threw things all out of kilter.

And that's when I realized that baseball was completely business. That there was no sentiment or loyalty involved at all.

And that was the first time I realized that baseball had become another form of show business. George felt that, despite whatever limitations Reggie might have had as a player, he was going to be the one to bring the people into the park. I never played to the crowd. I don't like to do it. I'm not comfortable doing it, and I don't even know whether I could play well under that kind of pressure. But Reggie could. He was one of the few guys who would put pressure on himself in order to play better. I usually don't acknowledge the crowd. When they yell at me from the stands, I figure if I yell back, then they are all going to know that I can hear them, and then they'll all be yelling. It's hard for me to concentrate while I'm in the field if I'm talking to the people in the stands.

Looking back on it, I probably should have done things a little differently. I should have made myself a lot more accessible to the press and gotten my name in the papers a lot more. Because, as I have found out since, that's how you make money in New York, by getting your name in the paper a lot. That's another way the game has changed. When I first came into baseball, you were paid based on your statistics, and on what you contributed to the team. Now, in the last seven or so years, it's how many times you can get your name in the paper for whatever you've done. The more controversial you are, or the more well-known you are, the more you're going to get paid. Maybe it would have been different if I had started in the Yankee organization. I might have been able to see that early on. But in Minnesota and Cleveland, you were paid just for what you did on the field, not for what you said. Once I got to New York, I could see that this had changed.

Reggie showed everyone the way. He wanted the headlines. He wanted the spotlight. And that was fine. Because there are a lot of us who don't, and he had a way of taking the pressure off the rest of us by being so visible. I felt, "Let him be the center of controversy, the center of attention. It makes it easier for the rest of us to play the game." In a way, I felt sorry for him a lot of times because of the problems he brought upon himself. He came to New York to create an image, and he did it.

He sold himself. He shouldn't complain about people hounding and bothering him, because that's what he wanted all along.

Reggie is very rude to people in public, because they don't leave him alone. But that's what he wanted. He didn't realize it would become so burdensome to have all those people around him all the time. That's the way he burst upon the New York scene, and that's the way he left—as the center of attention.

Today, my recommendation to a young ballplayer is, "Be controversial. Be as controversial as you can—if you can handle it." A lot of players can't. Reggie was one of the guys who could, and the more controversial he was, the better he played. Our kids, Mattingly or Balboni, they will never be controversial. All the young kids coming up are quiet. But I tell them, "Being a good soldier is only going to cost you money in the long run."

After assessing our '76 team, it seemed obvious to me that the position we needed to fill most was shortstop. I didn't think Jim Mason or Fred Stanley was our answer. Grich had been a second baseman. Perhaps he could have filled the bill. The player I thought we should have signed we didn't even draft: Joe Rudi. He would have helped us an awful lot. The guy we got we didn't even need: Reggie Jackson. We had Oscar Gamble in right, Mickey Rivers in center, Lou Piniella in left. As far as I could see, we didn't need another outfielder. We ended up having to trade Oscar to get Bucky Dent from Chicago. But George was happy, he got Reggie with his big bat and big mouth.

When the Yankees signed Jackson, his reputation preceded him. I had heard that wherever he went, he caused a commotion. Catfish said, "If you think things are controversial now, wait till Reggie starts his shit." Right away, he came out with his story that Munson couldn't lead the team worth a damn, that "I'm the straw that's gonna stir the drink." That's no way to come over to a new club, by downgrading the captain of the team. I thought it was a bunch of bull. When Catfish came over, he settled in very quietly and did his job and was great. Reggie had been over here for a week, and he's telling everybody how great he's going to be. New people on a ballclub should try to blend in before they let their personalities show. Reggie came on strong right from the start. It got him in bad with a lot of his teammates, because he was so outspoken right from the beginning.

That first week Thurman and Lou and I were looking at one another wondering, "What's this guy all about?" We had won the year before. We didn't need him and his flamboyance in order to win again. We didn't need the publicity that trails along behind him to win. Maybe George told him to do that, to be controversial. In any case, Reggie responded well to all the hoopla. Maybe he couldn't have played a passive role and still been productive. I never talked to him about it. The few times I tried, he always—within three or four sentences—would bring up how much money he was making doing this, how much money he was making doing that. He was very money conscious. Plus he had to be the center of conversation, all the time. You always had to be talking about him. I don't like to talk about money ever, and I don't like to be the center of attention, so I shied away from him for that reason more than anything.

He ended up being friends with Fran Healy and Mike Torrez. Reggie didn't have a whole lot of friends on the team. A lot of people kept him at arm's length because of all the controversy. He would say people didn't like him, because he was black, because he was making a lot of money. But it didn't have anything to do with those things. Wherever he went controversy surrounded him, and a lot of us shied away from him because of that. Thurman, in particular, was always wary of Reggie. It wasn't a great relationship, but what would you expect? Thurman had been the Most Valuable Player in the league the year before. Here was Reggie coming in and challenging the popular veteran. It didn't set well with any of us.

And what made our relationship with Reggie worse was that Reggie and George were buddy-buddy, and when George had a birthday party, he would invite Reggie and nobody else on the team. We would wonder, "What the hell is going on around here?" We would wonder, "Is this guy a player or is he front office? Why would the owner invite him and nobody else?" I know Billy felt very strongly about that. Billy likes to be numero uno, and he didn't like Reggie coming in and hogging the spotlight. When one of the minority owners quit, the guy said, "I don't want to be around here when those egos start clashing." And he was right. They certainly did clash.

The crazy times really began after Reggie announced he was the straw that stirred the drink, and of course Billy right away wanted Reggie to know that he, Billy, was the straw. And all the while, there was George, sitting in his office thinking he was stirring the drinks. I'll tell you, for a couple of years there, there was an awful lot of stirring going on. Something crazy was going on every single day.

And in one way, it was good for the rest of us, because it took the spotlight and put it somewhere else. I was able to come and go as I pleased. Reggie always had a story for the newspaper people. George always had a story. Or Billy did. Those three put on a show that was fascinating to watch from up close.

Billy is a very proud and stubborn man, and as manager he has only one law, really: he's the boss. He's the most important person in the dugout during the game. When Reggie came to the Yankees, Reggie was always a threat to Billy. Billy knew that Reggie and George were always palling around, and Billy also knew that George was always giving him, Billy, a hard time. To Billy, Reggie's being there wasn't all that different from George's being there. And everyone knows how Billy feels when George tries to tell him how to run the team.

In the first season Reggie was there, we were playing in Boston in June. Somebody hit a blooper out to right field, and Reggie went after it kind of tentatively and took his time throwing it in, and the batter hustled it into a double. Billy blew his cork, and he ordered Paul Blair to grab his glove and replace Reggie. I was standing by third base, and I could see what was coming. Our dugout was on the third-base side, and as Paul came trotting by me, he gave me a look like "Jesus Christ, watch this," and he went out there and tapped Reggie on the shoulder and told him he was replacing him. When Reggie got back to the dugout, I couldn't hear what he was saying to Billy, but I could see them jawing at each other and gesturing.

Something had been brewing inside Billy about Reggie, because Billy wouldn't have done that if it had been some other player. Billy decided to take it out on Reggie that day. And unfortunately it was on national television, and it made us look bad. And yet, that's the show-business aspect that George loves, and George undoubtedly loved it. "Here's my Yankees on national television getting as much exposure as they can." And then George added to the controversy by threatening to fire Billy over it.

Even though I was as close to everything going on as anyone, I still don't know the real reasons behind the incident. A lot of the players are very suspicious of George's motives when something like this happens. We figure to ourselves, "We don't know how he did it, but somehow George is behind it."

The Yankees are in competition with the Mets, and more than anything else George wants to put people in the seats. It's that simple. What would attract more attention than a Billy–Reggie feud? People only have so much money to spend on athletic events in New York, and if we were to go about things in a dull manner, the way the Mets do, then people wouldn't come out and watch us. If we can be real flamboyant, then people are going to pay their money to see us. The players may not like it, but after all these years we understand it.

If you're playing for the Yankees, you'd better be one of those players who can play amid all the distractions. We're out on the field concentrating on baseball, and George is up in his box concentrating on what he can do to make headlines. And he's real good at it. Last winter he got headlines over the Super Bowl. He has a great

knack for using the press. He knows how to upstage anybody whenever he wants. He might sign a free agent in
November, but he'll wait until the perfect time to grab a
headline to announce it.

I wasn't aware of this back in '77, but I understand it
far better now, and I try to explain it to the younger,
newer players on the Yankees. I say to them, "Don't
take what he says personally. It's just George's way of
getting the Yankees into the headlines." Or rather getting
George into the headlines.

I tried to tell it to Davey Collins last year. Poor Davey
got so flustered and upset playing here, he didn't know
what was going on. George gave him almost a million
dollars a year to play, and then never gave him a position.
Dave was a little unsure of himself, and when he read the
derogatory things George said about him, he was walking
around totally lost. Adding to Dave's problem last year
was that he didn't have a strong manager on his side. The
manager was George's puppet, so Dave didn't have
much choice but to go to another club. George says the
Yankees are run just like a business. In business sometimes you get screwed over. That's what happened to
Dave.

All through '77 Billy wanted to DH Reggie, and the
other players wanted him to DH as well. He was too
much of a liability out there on the field. Now I'm not
saying Reggie was a terrible outfielder. He never loafed.
He tried as hard as anybody. But his skills were not as
good as what we had on the bench. Our better outfielders
would be DH'ing, and Reggie would be in right, and it

didn't make any sense, except that that's what George wanted, and he owned the team. Reggie wanted to be seen for two hours a night, not ten minutes, so he could promote his candy bar, promote his line of clothes, promote his electronic equipment. And we resented him for that, because there's one thing a professional ballplayer can't abide, and that's a selfish teammate. The team should always come first, and I don't care who the hell you are. It bothered all of us, even a mild-mannered guy like Chambliss, who said in the papers, "When he puts himself in the outfield like that, he's not being a team player."

And yet no player ever went to Reggie to ask him to put the team first, because we all knew he would have taken it the wrong way. He was in New York to make a name for himself and he got away with it, because Reggie's being out there benefited George as much as it did Reggie.

With Reggie as a given and George as a given, Billy was the wrong person to have managing the team, because he had just as strong an ego as they did. I knew right from the start that it wasn't going to work for very long, and it didn't. The biggest drawback to having those three guys together was that it took away the fun for the rest of us. We had won in '76 with no controversy. And we had enough talent in '77 to win again, despite all the screaming. Maybe some of the guys liked it, but personally, I hated every minute of it. I could still look forward to the two or three hours when I could go out onto the field and play the game itself. Playing the games was still as much fun as always. And I was personally able to keep out of the line of fire, so it really didn't affect me. But I didn't enjoy reading what was written in the papers, and it got to be wearing as reporters circled around the clubhouse like vultures, waiting to pick Billy or Reggie apart.

And a side effect of all this was that Thurman became angry, because he was a guy who wanted his share of the headlines, and there just weren't enough to go around. One time he grew a beard and made some headlines. He knew it went against George's rules, and he also knew he would get Billy in trouble, but at the time he was angry at everyone, and he decided to piss both of them off. Thurman was very unhappy with the situation, and wanted to get sent to Cleveland to be closer to his home in Canton. I wish they had traded him like he wanted, because he'd probably be alive today. He wouldn't have had to take up flying. Because you have to remember that Thurman was the Most Valuable Player in 1976. He had led us to the American League pennant, and he was from the old school. He felt that you should be paid based on your accomplishments.

For myself, I really didn't mind playing with Reggie at all. I never played the game for the headlines. I always played the game for the sheer enjoyment of playing the game. Reggie was a productive player, and by being the center of attention all the time, he kept the press away from me and away from a lot of other players, and that made things easier for us.

Reggie used the reporters. They thought they were smarter than he was, but all the time it was Reggie who was using them. He'd tell them a story exactly the way he wanted it, and he would get his headlines, and it made him in New York.

Of course, while Reggie was doing his thing, the one who was suffering the most was Billy. Billy has always been loyal to me, and I've always considered him a friend, so I felt very bad for Billy. He brings a lot of his problems on himself. That's the way he is, stubborn and unbending, and any time you have a personality like that you're going to get hurt. Billy's problem was that he had the attention of the nation on him, and he would leave himself open to guys like Henry Hecht. It was bound to happen that sooner or later Henry would nail Billy, because when Billy was feeling the pressure, sometimes he would have a pop or two and say things he shouldn't. That's what happened when he said, "One's a born liar, and the other's convicted." It was Billy's fault that he said it. But those two guys, Hecht and Murray Chass of the *Times,* never should have printed it. And the only reason Chass printed it was that he knew Hecht certainly would run it, and he would look bad if Hecht printed it and he didn't. Billy never should have been fired. Never. But he was, because the writers don't like him, and they allowed Billy to sandbag himself. And I will never, ever forgive them for it.

After leading us to a pennant in '76, Billy took us all the way in '77. We played the Dodgers in the World Series, and no matter how negatively some of us may have felt about Reggie, when I think back, it was Reggie's three home runs in the final game that overshadowed everything else. It was probably the greatest single-game performance by a player I've ever seen. It was amazing. It was the sixth and final game, and it gave me chills when he hit that third one, which was hit even farther than the first two. It was into the back seats in center field, where only a couple other balls have been hit. There was electricity in the air, and you could just feel that it was going to be Reggie's day. It was magic. And it didn't matter in the slightest whether you liked him or detested him. You put away whatever you felt for the guy and just bathed in the magnitude of the achievement. He was my teammate, and I was pulling for him, and so was each and every guy in that Yankee dugout. We were overjoyed that he could have a day like that.

There are a lot of people who don't understand that a professional ballplayer can hate a guy's guts and still root for him. Not that I hated Reggie's guts. I didn't at all, but how you feel about the guy dressing next to you has no bearing on what goes on on that field, because if he does well, and a few other guys do well, that means you're going to win, and that means money in your pocket. I was very happy for Reggie. I was happy for all of us.

I remember the cheers. After the third home run, I walked out to the on-deck circle as the crowd was cheering and cheering, and I took my helmet off and waved at everybody as though they were cheering me, and I enjoyed my little fantasy as the noise swirled over the whole stadium. Then I kneeled down in the on-deck circle as Reggie continued to stand out there and wave, and I applauded too.

JULY 1983

Steve Howe turned himself in to a drug rehabilitation clinic, and the Dodgers responded by fining him $54,000. This isn't exactly the way to get other players with drug problems to seek help. It was his second offense, so what the Dodgers are telling their players is, "If you think you're going to need help a second time, you better not ask for it." That's going to keep players from turning themselves in a second time. Or probably even a first time.

It's not that I don't see the Dodgers' point. I do. They're saying, "Because of your problem, you've been out a month. We're not going to pay you for a month." But as far as getting other guys to turn themselves in for treatment, which should be the most important thing, that huge fine is the stupidest thing they could have done. Nobody is going to believe Don Newcombe when he comes around to spring training camps and says, "If you have a drug or drinking problem, we'll help you."

When a player has a problem, it's supposed to be kept secret, and it just isn't. The first thing that happens, the club goes right to the papers. Like Neil Allen of the Mets. Neil confided in the Mets management he thought he had a drinking problem. Immediately, management leaked it to the newspapers. The next day management made a public statement saying that Allen didn't have a drinking problem, but it had already been in all the papers that he did have one. The Mets could have handled it quietly, and not taken away Allen's dignity.

As a player, I can't help but think that for whatever reason, the club deliberately tried to make the player look bad. A ballclub has only one thing going for it: its ballplayers. Why would a club want a player to look bad? That's why I never can understand why George does some of the things he does to publicly ridicule his players. People don't pay to watch his office workers type. They only pay to watch ballplayers play. So why downgrade your only assets?

We were in the players' lounge watching the Game of the Week on television—the Cardinals against the Dodgers. The Cardinals had a couple of admitted problem guys with Darrell Porter and Lonnie Smith, and the Dodgers had a few with Howe and Bob Welch. We figured, "Don Newcombe must be having a busy day today. He must be sitting behind home plate, halfway between the dugouts, yelling, 'Who needs me the most?' "

We played a four-game series against the Red Sox, and in the first three games they scored eight, ten, and seven runs. We managed to win the first one, when we scored seven runs in the second inning. They came back and tied it up, but we ended up winning the game. That game tells you something about this new statistic, the game-winning RBI. What a farce it is! All it shows is who drives in the go-ahead run, assuming your pitching can hold them. If the pitching doesn't hold them, your RBI is lost. It's such a totally meaningless statistic.

I opened up the scoring of that game by hitting a home run. Then I came up later in the inning and doubled in the seventh run. Because our pitching couldn't hold them, they tied it up at seven. Roy hit a sacrifice fly to make it eight to seven, and I came up later and drove in the tenth and eleventh runs, so I had the first, seventh, tenth, and eleventh runs, and we won the game twelve to eight, and Smalley was the one who got the game-winning RBI.

We weren't so lucky in the second game. It was one of those games. As the Red Sox were running around the bases, I was standing out there just hoping we would get a break. In some games, the other team gets a couple of cheap hits, and it snowballs. You just hope someone in the bullpen can get up fast and get ready fast and maybe stop them. And when the reliever comes in and doesn't do any better, you write it off. Just one of those games. Which is why you're so glad there are 162 games. The game ends, and you forget about it immediately.

As a player you'd just as soon get beat sixteen to two as two to one, because the other team might have worn itself out scoring those sixteen runs. I don't want to get beat sixteen to two, because the earned run averages of the pitchers go way up, but you can accept that kind of defeat a lot easier than a two to one. In a two to one game, you can always think of two or three things you might have done differently to perhaps win the game. When you lose sixteen to two, you know there was nothing you could have done about it.

After getting beat badly in two games, Shane Rawley went out there and gave up seven runs, but pitched eight and two-thirds innings, and even though he got beat, it was a gutsy performance, 'cause it gave the bullpen a rest. Everyone really appreciated what he did.

In the fourth game of the series against the Red Sox, Dave Righetti pitched a no-hitter.

In the game he pitched against Baltimore right before the no-hitter, he shut out the Orioles seven to nothing and didn't walk a batter. That was his first major league shutout. And his next time out, he pitched the no-hitter.

That was some game. I was really into that game, even though I wasn't playing. After the first inning, I said, "I think Rags really has it today. I'll bet he gets thirteen strikeouts." In the first three innings, he must have had seven. I sensed that he was going to give an extraordinary performance. He was overpowering them. Right away, when you see that, you know it's going to be special, but the possibility of a no-hitter didn't enter my mind until the seventh inning.

The bench is an interesting place from which to watch a game like that. After every inning, Dave walked back from the dugout to the clubhouse. The clubhouse is a lot cooler, a lot quieter. It takes away some of the nervousness. That day, he was aware of the no-hitter from the first inning on. After the game he said the only teammate who said anything to him was me.

After the seventh inning, I went up to the clubhouse to join him, and I asked him whether he had packed for our trip. He and I were going down to Atlantic City for the all-star break. We were leaving from the ballpark. I just casually asked him, ''Are you packed for the trip, or are you going to go home first?'' He said, ''We'll go home first.'' Afterward he said that was the only thing anyone said to him during the entire game. Everyone was afraid to make the wrong comment, afraid to break his concentration. I figured it wouldn't hurt to ask him if he was packed for the trip.

I was pulling for him especially hard that day because my family was out on the West Coast, and I wasn't able to go out for the break. Everybody else had made plans, and Rags didn't have anything else to do, so the day before that July Fourth, we decided, what the hell, we'll go down to Atlantic City and bury ourselves on the beach. I was hoping for a good performance by him that day so he'd be in a good mood.

It was the first no-hitter I've ever seen. In the ninth, everyone on the bench was edgy. With no one out and a man on first, we almost made a double play, but the throw pulled the first baseman off the bag. We figured, "Oh, no, something bad's going to happen." Because I've seen that many times. The next guy popped up, and because we didn't get the double play, Rags had to face this guy Boggs, who was leading the league in average and hits, and who doesn't strike out very often. He's a singles hitter, a contact hitter who sprays the ball all over the park, the last guy you would want up in a situation like that. You'd rather see one of their big sluggers come up, guys he had been blowing the ball by all afternoon.

He took Boggs to two and two and threw him a great slider and struck him out, and all hell broke loose. I was standing on the top step of the dugout. I was more nervous than if I had been playing. When you're playing you can take out some of your aggression. When you're on the bench there is nothing you can do.

Rags had planned on driving his Bronco down to Atlantic City. I was going to sit back and relax. After that game, I told him, "I'll drive. You relax." He had earned that. I followed him over to his apartment in Washington Heights, and Jerry Azar from Channel 7 was following us. I parked outside the apartment, while Dave put his gear away and packed his vacation clothes. Azar was apologetic. He said, "I'm sorry, but I was told by our news department to follow Dave wherever he goes all night. What are you guys doing? You having a party here?'' I said, ''No, we're going to Atlantic City.'' He said, ''Atlantic City? I can't follow you all the way down there.'' I said, ''Great.''

We stayed at Bally's at Park Place and registered under my name, and it was a good thing. If we had registered under his, they would have found us. People were looking for him for a couple of days, and all he wanted to do was get away. I didn't have a very good time. The reason I hadn't played in that game was that I had a bad case of what I thought was conjunctivitis, pinkeye. I woke up that morning and my eye had crusted shut, so there was no way I could have played.

The whole time I was down there, my eye was so sensitive to bright light, I couldn't sit on the beach. I couldn't do much at all.

We went to see a couple shows. We saw David Brenner and then Sheckie Green. Dave was introduced, but he's a very, very shy kid who doesn't want the limelight. Other guys would have stayed around New York and milked it, going on every talk show. I'm sure he could have written his ticket right then. But all he wanted to do was get away, and if that's what he wanted, he couldn't have picked a better time. When his agent called and told him of all the offers, he said, ''We'll take care of them after the season.'' He told me, ''I got another game to pitch in four days, and I got to be ready for it. I can't let this thing get out of hand.'' For a twenty-four-year-old kid, he had things very much under control.

* * *

It was a shame Rags didn't get to pitch in the all-star game. He would have been a fabulous attraction, pitching right after his no-hitter. Ron Guidry originally was supposed to represent the Yankees at the all-star game, but then Gator hurt himself and the American League manager didn't pick Righetti to replace him. He picked Tippy Martinez. Dave was upset. I know he was. The American League people had asked him if he could go three innings. He said he probably could. It was a stupid question to ask, because the only ones who go three in those games are the starters, and they weren't looking for him to start. The relievers only have to come in and throw an inning. He pitched Monday, and it would have been his day to throw between starts two days later, so they should have picked him. Rags deserved to go.

Last year, the Yankees had five pitching coaches, and the guy who suffered the most was Righetti. They tried to change his delivery, mess with his motion, and he was such a mixed-up kid he ended up for a little while back at Columbus. Well, now he's shown them all.

After Rags pitched his no-hitter, he started telling reporters how terrific Art Fowler had been with him. That's the Art Fowler who George and Henry Hecht say doesn't know anything about pitching. Guidry says he's dedicating the rest of the season to Art, and Rags says Art helped him so much, and yet George got mad at Billy and fired Art. It doesn't make any sense, but that's the way things are run around here.

Art is not a great teacher of pitching, but he instills confidence in guys like Rags and Guidry. Once you get to the big leagues, the teaching should have been done. That's why the whole structure of the minor leagues is all fouled up. The guys who should be doing the important teaching are the guys in the A and Double-A leagues, and they're the ones making the least money. They're the ones who should be making the most money. It's the same way outside baseball. Teachers make peanuts compared to people in other professions. Our priorities are somewhat screwed up.

I haven't talked to Billy about Art because it might set him off. I know how upset Billy was.

George is this kind of guy: he gave Art a twenty-thousand-dollar bonus and said, "Here, Art, you're fired." You don't know what to do. How can you get mad at a guy who just handed you twenty grand? You don't get mad until you get home. You say, "What the hell am I doing here? I just got fired." George does that a lot. He fires people, and he has some feelings of remorse about it, so he throws in some money.

After he fired Art, he brought in Sammy Ellis. He was at Columbus. And he had been up with us for a while. It's funny. After Rags' no-hitter, I told Sammy Ellis, "You don't know it, but the last time Rags almost threw a no-hitter, also against Boston, Stan Williams, the pitching coach, got fired. You don't know how close you were to being fired today." Sammy laughed.

George may have hurt us badly by getting rid of Art. Because Billy doesn't trust Torborg and Ellis, he's decided to make all the pitching decisions. In two games in a row, he left Guidry in to go the distance when he was way behind. Billy's feeling is, "He's pitching well, and he should get the chance to win if he can." But I think Billy should take him out early in games like that and rest his arm. He might be stronger in September if he got a couple more innings' rest in the warm weather. There's no percentage in letting him stay in there five runs down in the seventh inning. He's pitched five complete games in a row. I hope it doesn't take its toll later in the year.

I can tell when Guidry isn't as sharp as usual. Usually it's in the beginning of the game. I'll walk over to him and say, "Gid, what was that that guy hit?" He'll say, "Nothing." I'll say, "What was it, a fastball or a slider?" He'll say, "Nothing." "What do you mean? Was it a fastball?" "I don't have a fastball yet." "As your third baseman," I'll say, "I'd like to know whether you have good stuff or not. Whether to play my position or go hide behind the tarp."

Sometimes at the beginning of the game he has absolutely nothing, and he'll say, "That was a nothing pitch." Sometimes he gets by with it, and then as the game goes on, he gets stronger and stronger.

When he tires, Guidry should say to Billy, "Take me out," but Guidry would never do that. A couple years ago, George was criticizing Ronnie for not being able to complete games. He said Guidry wasn't big enough to be a nine-inning pitcher. So that's another reason why Ronnie wouldn't come out if his arm was falling off.

The pitchers are going to have to take it upon themselves to tell Billy when they want to come out. If Billy says, "Are you all right? Do you want to continue?" they are going to have to be honest with him. They're aware of what Billy did at Oakland a couple years ago. He left the starting pitchers in until their arms fell off. It's their careers. They can't afford to be scared of Billy.

I wasn't upset about not being on the all-star team. George Brett, Doug De Cinces, and Wade Boggs are having better years than I am. Boggs is leading the league in hitting at .360, and he didn't even make the team. I'm not having an all-star–type year.

It really doesn't bother us that the American League hasn't won the all-star game in eleven years, except when we have to keep answering the same question: "When are you guys going to win one?" Or "Why does the National League keep beating you?" Fans don't understand that it's just an exhibition game. It isn't even played like a regular baseball game. Whoever heard of a pitcher coming out after three innings after he struck out six or seven guys? Or retired nine men in a row? That's not the way baseball is played. As a result, the players can't take it too seriously. I say play it like a regular game. Play nine guys the whole way if you want. Why do you have to use twenty-five guys? Make it a real game, and then you'll see who has the best players.

Don't get me wrong. The players at the game care who wins. They try their hardest to win, but it doesn't break their hearts to lose. They don't drop a game in the standings. Sure you'd like to win, if only so everyone'll stop asking those questions about beating the National League. But if they are going to make such an issue out of it, let's make it like a real game. Let the starting pitcher go seven or eight innings, let your regular players play the whole game, like a regular season game.

Rags and I got back from Atlantic City in time to watch the all-star game. I had to listen to it. My eyes were so sore, I couldn't even keep them open. I had that thing for five days. Even after the break, I had to miss the first game with Kansas City. I went to an eye doctor there, and he told me I was allergic to the medication the trainer gave me, and he gave me another medicine, and my eyes cleared up in a couple hours. They had thought it was pinkeye, but it turned out to be a virus. The doctor said, "It can start from a sore throat," and I thought back, and I remembered that I had had a sore throat the day before I got this infection.

To play 162 games, you have to stay healthy, and it's not easy. And it's important to stay healthy, if only to save the trainers from George. Every time someone gets hurt, George calls the trainers on the carpet. If a guy runs head-first into a wall, it's the trainer's fault. Every time there's an injury, Gene Monahan knows he's going to get a phone call and get chewed out. And there's not a thing Monahan can say except "Yes sir. No sir. Yes sir. No sir. I'll do my best."

In 1978 George put the trainers on probation. George owns horses, and he's rough on those trainers too. He's always hiring and firing trainers and jockeys. He feels that if he hires a trainer, that guy should be able to get someone well within a day or two. The healing process takes longer than that.

We lost two out of three to the Twins in Minnesota, and it wasn't much fun. We had played well in Kansas City, and then boom, we went flat. It could have been the Twins' ballpark. Even though it's supposed to be a hitter's park, I don't see the ball well there at all. Everything looks yellow, has a funny tint to it. The ball's right on top of you before you see it, and if you hit the ball in the air, there's a good chance the outfielder won't see it, because when the ball gets above the lights it disappears. Every game, there are two or three popups or fly balls where everyone stands around looking up and can't see them. And when the ball hits, it starts bouncing, and it seems like it jumps higher with each bounce. The field isn't Astroturf. I don't know what you call it, but it's real soft and spongy. The ball bounces in front of me, and sometimes it bounces right over my head and comes down in the outfield somewhere. It's not good baseball. It's just not the same game we were taught to play. It's the worst stadium in the league. Because it's enclosed, it would be a nice, comfortable place to watch a football game, but for baseball it's not very good.

I heard the Twins are going to be leaving there after a year anyway—they're supposed to be moving to Tampa. Calvin Griffith has a clause in his contract stating that if attendance drops below an average of 1.4 million a year over three years he may leave. I doubt that he draws that much in three years. Calvin isn't as rich as George or Gene Autry or the guys from Oakland, but I never feel sorry for him. You can tell just by looking at him that he's making enough money to get his meals. He's not skimping on the grocery bills, that's for sure. He's from another generation. Baseball has passed him by. He's so cheap. And yet he had his brothers on the payroll, they were called vice-presidents, and they were making more money than Harmon Killebrew and Tony Oliva. That doesn't make for a very happy atmosphere. It's a nice town, but it's just too bad they have Calvin for an owner.

Minnesota drafted me out of college. At the time I didn't know anything about the different organizations, and I didn't know how cheap the Twins were compared to other organizations. About the best at that time was the Red Sox, and now they are probably the worst because of all the turmoil going on up there, with Buddy LeRoux and Haywood Sullivan fighting for ownership.

I discovered how cheap the Twins were when I played

for them in 1968. I got called up for the last month of the season, and I hit five home runs my first four days up. The Twins weren't going anywhere. We were twenty-two games out of first place. But here was this rookie who hit four home runs in three games against Detroit, and Detroit won the pennant that year, and it was my thinking that I was drawing some people pretty good—perhaps they were coming out just to see this new phenom. So the next year, when contract time came up, I was offered ten thousand dollars, which was the minimum salary, and I wrote back and said I wanted eleven thousand dollars. I was figuring that my home runs must have made him an extra thousand dollars. And he sent me a nasty telegram: "If you think you have any chance of making the ballclub, you better get your ass to spring training and right now." So what could I do? I reported and played for the minimum. At that point I saw that unless you were Calvin's flesh and blood, you weren't going to see any real money. His brothers would get the raises, but he wouldn't pay his players.

The grumbling among the players about Calvin was terrible. I don't know of a single player who liked playing for him. If there had been free agency at that time, you would have seen everyone jumping to other clubs just so for the first time they could get paid what they were worth. Killebrew was there a long, long time, and I don't think he ever made a hundred thousand dollars. Oliva never made that much either. And yet Calvin's brother, the vice-president in charge of concessions, was making big money. It was not a fun situation.

And even though I went from Minnesota to Cleveland, which was another cheap organization, because Cleveland was going broke at the time and Stouffer, the owner, didn't have any money to spend, I was still glad to get away from Calvin. There were other guys, like Charley Manual and Rick Rennick, who were there the same time I was, and those guys didn't get traded. They got lost in the shuffle, sent back to the minor leagues, and they never got much of a chance.

What's amazing about Calvin is that the list of players who left him could fill the roster of an all-star team—guys like Carew, Wynegar, Lyman Bostock, and Smalley. But the Twins are still competitive because they keep coming up with good, young kids from their minor league system. They keep them for six years, and then they become free agents, and leave. But for the first five years they are stuck there in Minnesota. A lot of people talk about how bad the Twins are, and yet they aren't looking at it right. In truth, it's amazing the Twins do as well as they do considering the number of players Calvin allows to get away. There are ex-Twins on teams all over the league. The only other team that has that many of its players spread around the majors is the Yankees.

Every time we play Texas, the rumors start: Buddy Bell is coming to New York. I know George would like to have him, but I don't know if Buddy would want to come here with this atmosphere. Buddy is a pretty easy-going guy.

Last year John Denny was a pitcher for Cleveland who played out his option and then was drafted by the Yankees. He said, "I just don't want to play for Steinbrenner. I don't want to play for that man." It was refreshing to hear someone say, "You can keep your money. I'll stay here in Cleveland." As a reward, he got traded to Philadelphia, so everything worked out fine for the guy. I remember Denny in 1981. We had a fight with him, because he threw at Reggie, and Reggie homered, and when he crossed home plate he charged the mound, and they got into a brawl. George said he was going to sue Denny right there in the Bronx court. And then at the end of the year he ended up drafting him. And then he can't understand why Denny doesn't want to come here and play for him. Sometimes the way George goes about things doesn't make sense.

Ray Fontenot came to the Yankees in that botched-up deal that sent Mickey Rivers to Texas and brought Oscar Gamble back here. Ray was just a throw-in at the time. He had only played a year of ball, but the first time I saw him I could tell he was going to be a pretty good pitcher. He's a Tommy-John–type, keeps the ball low and throws a lot of ground balls. Seems to have a pretty good head on his shoulders. He gave up a couple of monster home runs to Greg Luzinski over in Chicago, but he came right back his next start and pitched well. When that happens to some guys, it demoralizes them. We faced a kid from Toronto, Williams. It was his first big league game against the Yankees. And we hit him for three home runs and five runs in five innings. He threw everything hard, and those are the pitchers we hit the best. We didn't win because Toronto scored ten runs and beat us, but the kid may still be shook up, because he started a second game against us, and he didn't get anybody out. He faced five hitters, gave up a grand slam home run and then another home run. He surely had that weighing on his mind for a week.

Fontenot, on the other hand, gave up the home runs to Luzinski—one of them was over the roof in Chicago—and lost, and he came right back and pitched a couple of excellent games. Fontenot got a fan letter. It was a computer printout, and it must have had the words "Walk Luzinski" on it two or three hundred times. Ray showed it to everybody. There was a little note on the bottom, "The next time you pitch against Chicago, I hope this helps." He's got a good head on his shoulders. He can take a good ass-kicking and still come back and pitch well.

Take guys like Jim Beattie, Mike Morgan, Ken Clay, Jay Howell. They have or had great stuff. But they

couldn't win here. Jay Howell right now. He has great
stuff, and it's a mystery to all of us why he isn't winning.
Maybe it's a break for Fontenot that George is in one of
his quieter periods. He didn't come down on him for allowing Luzinski to hit those home runs. In years past
George might have made headlines by saying, "Who is
this guy Fontenot? What's he doing in the majors?" But
lately, he's been quiet.

Bowie Kuhn finally made a correct decision. He finally made one good decision for the good of baseball.
He resigned. We were up in Toronto at the time. We had
lost a game, and somebody asked me about it. I said, "It
was too hard to play baseball with such an important
event as Bowie quitting. It was on my mind all night."

Bowie was such a farce. Who cares whether he's commissioner or not? Whoever they elect, or whatever committee runs it, has to be much better than that clown.

My dislike for him goes back to problems I had in
winter ball in 1971. I got kicked out of Venezuela. Five
of us—Chuck Brinkman, Billy Wynne, Tony Muser, a
pitcher named Jerry Cramm, and I were accused of
throwing a game.

We had asked our owner for more money because we
had gotten into the playoffs. I was playing for Aragua in a
town called Maracay. All the other teams were giving

their American players extra money to stay for the play-offs. We asked our owner, and he said, "No, it's against the rules." So we didn't really press the issue. But somehow he thought that if we didn't get that money, we weren't going to try. In the next game, I hit into a double play my first time up, so he thought I did it on purpose. The owner was a banker who didn't understand baseball. Our first baseman, Muser, made an error, and the owner thought he did that on purpose. He went to the newspapers and radio. And he got everyone riled up against us, and we were told to get out of the country.

Two days after the incident, the owner realized he was wrong. It was explained that part of baseball is hitting into double plays, people make errors.

When I got back I wrote Bowie Kuhn a letter telling him exactly what happened, and I never heard one word back from him. Our names were never cleared. I lost all respect for him right then, because he never even tried to take up our side. At the time I had been in the major leagues three years.

There were other things he did, or rather didn't do. Where was he during the strike? On vacation. Peter Gammons of the *Boston Globe* wrote, "If Bowie Kuhn were still alive, this strike never would have happened." And that's the way I felt about it. What did Bowie Kuhn ever do for the good of baseball? He did everything for the good of certain owners, and that's all. To me he was nothing. I remember his name, Kuhn, because it rhymes with buffoon. I don't think anybody in the game of baseball is going to miss him.

* * *

I was upset that Mickey Mantle wasn't at the Old-Timers' Game this year. It isn't an Old-Timers' Game without Mickey. It's just silly. He could have come, even though Bowie barred him from baseball, but it was Mickey's way of showing Bowie Kuhn that he was a jerk. A lot of people go to Old-Timers' Day basically to see Mickey. I don't think they come to see Joe DiMaggio, because a lot of people didn't grow up with Joe Di-Maggio. They grew up with Mickey Mantle. They wanted to come back and see Mickey and Whitey and Maris. It's a shame. Mickey took a stand against Bowie Kuhn's decision, and I respect him for it.

The Old-Timers' Game itself is kind of a sad exhibition when you see a bunch of old men running around out there. A couple years ago a batter hit a nice little two-hop ground ball at Phil Rizzuto, and it hit him in the nose and bloodied it. I don't enjoy seeing a bunch of old people who I once thought of as stars out there making fools of themselves. But if they're having a good time, it's worth it, and maybe when I get to that stage, I'll think it's worth it too. It's like Sparky Lyle said when he came back. "I always thought these games were a pain in the ass. The clubhouse was always filled with people. But now that I'm an old-timer, I love it." So maybe I'll have that feeling, too.

You have to share a locker with an old-timer, so Sparky and I shared my locker, since it used to be his. He was proud of what I had done with it. I have a beach chair, my own coffee pot. It's the biggest locker in the locker room.

BALLS

Sparky had been advertised by the Yankees on the radio and television as coming to the Old-Timers' Game. After *The Bronx Zoo* came out, George said, "We will never invite him back to Yankee Stadium," etcetera, and here are the ads: "Come back and see Sparky Lyle on Old-Timers' Day." Makes you wonder when George says something, whether he really means it.

My personal favorite old-timer is Roger Maris. We wore the same number. We were both home-run hitters. I get a kick out of seeing Roger. Mickey and Whitey I see during spring training, but Roger only comes for the Old-Timers' Day. I get my picture taken with him, get some autographed balls for my kids. It'll mean something to them someday. I've been told we have similar swings. Maybe Pete Sheehey, the clubhouse man, noticed that when he handed me Roger's old number when I first got here. I was wearing 12 at Cleveland. He gave me 9, which I thought was quite a tribute.

Against Minnesota at the stadium I dove to my right toward the third base line for a ball, but the ball took a bad hop and came back at me, and as I turned my body to make the catch, I landed on my elbow and jammed my right shoulder. It's the same problem I had at the end of last year. It's something all fouled up in the joint.

The thing is really sore. When I bring my arm back, I

feel like there's a knife sticking right into the shoulder. The trainer works on it, and after about ten throws, it feels all right, but at lunch I could hardly cut a piece of meat. And it was a good piece of meat too.

I knew as soon as I landed on it that I had hurt it. I threw the ball, and I couldn't even watch the throw. Billy took me out of the game. I didn't play for a couple of days. Now it's just a matter of playing through the pain. I can't afford to sit out with a sore shoulder at this point. A week of rest might help, but then a week of rest might throw everything else off, and it might take a while to get back in shape. I've made a couple of erratic throws because of it, but I just have to block it out of my mind and keep on going.

Every time I swing at a ball, if I stop my swing, it really bothers me. It's okay when I take a full swing, but if I have to decide whether to check the swing and feel the pain or go ahead and swing fully, I swing even though I know I shouldn't. Once the game gets going it gets loosened up. It's just something I'll have to live with.

I hurt the shoulder last year diving to the right side for a ball. It was the first part of September. It's something I can't get away from doing. It's an instinctive thing. I've thought, "Maybe I shouldn't dive for the ball," but I just have to do it.

I guess I take my ability to dive for balls and come up with the throw for granted. I often wonder why most of the other third basemen don't dive the way I do, and I really don't have an answer. When you dive through the air, your first thought is catching the ball, and then when you've caught it, your next thought is to get up immediately and make the throw as quickly as possible. Some guys can dive, but they get up slowly and then plant their feet and miss the runner by two steps. When I hit the ground, I want to try to bounce up as quickly as possible and throw the ball from down low. I don't want to have to stand straight up to throw it. That wastes too much time.

I can do it, so to me it's no big deal. Some guys just cannot do it. Maybe in the back of their minds they are afraid of getting hurt.

There's no trick to it. It's just a knack. You can't practice it. I never dive for balls in practice, because if you go after balls a hundred percent in practice, you end up hurting yourself. It's not a play to practice, and I would never advise anyone to practice it.

I've seen Ozzie Smith of the Cardinals. He dives, and he bounces up like he's on a trampoline and makes the throw. He doesn't have a strong, strong arm, but he gets up quick and gets rid of the ball quick.

I never saw Clete Boyer play, but I've been told he would dive for balls and throw runners out from his knees. I've tried that a few times this year, and a couple times got the guy out. I prefer to get up and throw. Boyer's arm was much stronger than mine, but I feel if I can get up quickly, I'll make the out, because I've always been very accurate.

To make the dive down the line, you have to have good anticipation. I anticipate that every ball is going to be hit either to one side of me or to the other. I envision it in my mind before every pitch. I picture the ball being hit, both ten feet to the left and ten feet to the right. I never expect the ball to be hit right at me. As the pitcher winds up, I see the batter hitting the ball over the bag or into the hole and me diving for it. I'm ready to go either way. I'll have already rehearsed it in my mind, so it doesn't surprise me when it happens.

I know that some players envision the ball hit at them, and they are ready for that, but they don't envision it hit ten feet to either side. As a result, they don't get a good jump on it.

Billy is on edge these days. He's snapping at coaches, and he's been kind of gruff. He's always been very rough on his coaches. He needs to yell at somebody just to let his frustrations out. He gets so much pressure from George. Whenever Billy yelled at Art, Art understood, because they had been together so long, and he knows how Billy is. And after Billy finished yelling, Art was able to talk to Billy and settle him down. Billy just hasn't been the same since George fired Art.

Coaches like Torborg and Sammy Ellis and Don Zimmer have no sway with Billy. Those guys were picked by George. They aren't coaches Billy wanted, and Billy doesn't trust them. I don't know how these coaches feel, because they would never say anything to a player. Most of our coaches have been managers, and they know what causes dissension, which is talking behind the manager's back. If they had any resentments, they would hold them in.

As far as the players are concerned, Billy is doing his job well. I mean, there are some players who aren't going to like him, players who aren't playing, but I don't think there are any guys saying, "I want to go somewhere else." There are some guys who are grumbling. Dave Righetti told Bob Shirley, "You spend more minutes in the penalty box than Dave Schultz." Billy's penalty box. Because Billy banished Shirley to the bullpen. He's been in Billy's doghouse forever. I'm sure guys like Shirley are upset that they aren't getting more of a chance.

Fans think, "Why should a guy like Shirley be upset? He's making good money." Still, everybody has his pride, wants to pitch well, wants his teammates to respect him. And if a guy doesn't get to play, he doesn't get that.

We had a fiasco the other day, the day that Randolph came back on the active list. We had to get rid of somebody. About two hours before the game they asked Larry Milbourne to go to Columbus. Milbourne said, "Let me go home and think about it." He went home. In the meantime, the front office—George and the new general manager, Murray Cook—decided that instead of Milbourne they wanted Campaneris off the roster. They decided to disable Campaneris with a mysterious wrist injury and keep Milbourne.

I came into the dugout after the first inning of the game against Detroit, looked around, walked back into the clubhouse, and Campaneris was sitting there out of uniform. I said to myself, "They must have put Campaneris on the disabled list." When I went back to the dugout, I looked around for Milbourne, and he wasn't around either. I said to Billy, "What was the final decision? What was our roster move today?" Billy said, "They put Campy on the disabled list, and they're keeping Milbourne." I said, "Well, where the hell is Milbourne?" Billy looked around and said, "I don't know." I said, "I was just up in the clubhouse, and he's not there. Goddamn, Billy, we're in the middle of a game, and we're short an infielder." Smalley was hurt, and he wasn't going to be able to play. We were really short. So Billy had Oscar call Milbourne at the hotel where he was staying. "Hey, you're still on the team. Get back to the park." About the sixth inning Larry got back to the ballpark, got in uniform, and sat on the bench the rest of the game. But it was a farce. There's such a lack of communication, you're left wondering, "What's going on around here?" You'd think on the New York Yankees things would be run more professionally.

And then when they brought Griffey back, someone else had to go, and it was Bye Bye Balboni. That's why we call him "Bye Bye," because we're always saying "Bye Bye." He was up with us for a month, and when he returned to the International League, he was still leading that league in home runs! By a lot. For his sake, I wish they would trade him and get him to an organization where he could play. The guy's going to hit forty home runs for somebody. Which is what George is afraid of. Bones is stuck between a rock and a hard place. There's no place for him to play for us, and they're afraid of looking bad if they get rid of him.

You can't take Don Mattingly out of the lineup. He's hitting .330 and playing great. Mattingly is one of our better players right now. We're making our stretch drive, and Mattingly is one of the guys leading the team. We have so much hitting talent, it's hard to see how we can lose the division.

The Yankees called up Barry Evans from Columbus, and he refused to report. I couldn't believe that. His wife was going to have a baby, and he didn't want to come up. He just about shot down his whole career right there. When you get a black mark against you like that, you're ruined in this organization, and who knows what other organizations will think. It doesn't make much sense to me. Even if he knew he was coming up just to sit, once he's here for one day, he gets on the medical plan until opening day of next season. If his wife is going to have a baby, that would have paid for all the expenses. Just that free medical plan alone should be enough for a guy to want to come to the big leagues. But he refused to report. So they sent Bobby Meacham up. Bobby didn't know what was going on either. First he heard that Barry was coming up, and then they told him he was coming. He got into one game.

In a late inning they hit a ball to him, and he booted it, and then with men on first and third, the winning run on third, he made a diving play up the middle, lay on the ground, and with a backhand flip, threw to second for the forceout. It saved the game for us. For some reason, after many years of having no rookies on the big club, some of the kids are finally making it up. Billy is a firm believer in bringing along a couple of rookies every year. My first year with him in Minnesota in '69, we had seven or eight rookies on the team. Billy likes to find an unknown rookie and push him. He did it in Texas, where he found catcher Jim Sundberg and first baseman Mike Hargrove. He found a couple kids at Oakland and let them play. And I think he would like to get some credit for doing that with the Yankees. He likes Meacham an awful lot as a player. He liked him in spring training. He would like to get credit for giving this kid his start in the big leagues.

Now that Andre Robertson has finally got his chance, he has done marvelously for us at shortstop. Andre has fantastic range. The only thing that could screw him up is their switching him back and forth between second and short. That might hurt his arm. The shortstop has to throw overhand. A second baseman usually throws sidearm. Once they leave him at short, he's going to be a great one.

And now that we have Larry Milbourne to fill in at second, Billy will be able to leave the kid at short. Where that leaves Roy I don't know, because I know that Billy doesn't like him at third. His hands are all right. He catches any balls hit at him, but again, the problem is his range. It takes him a while to get started after balls. Even when I don't play, Billy has Campaneris at third.

During Righetti's no-hitter Billy played Smalley at short, Robertson at second, and Campaneris at third. A lot of us thought he had all three playing out of position. We thought he should have had Campy at second, Robertson at short, and Smalley at third. And we ended up getting a no-hitter out of it. But this leads me to believe that Billy isn't too high on Smalley as a third baseman. He wants to keep him either at short or at first.

⬲

Baylor hasn't been a big part of this team, and only now is he beginning to fit in. It has taken him a while to get used to not being in the lineup all 162 games. Once in a while Billy might feel that someone else might be a better designated hitter, and he might play Oscar or Piniella, and it's taken Baylor half a season to learn to live with that.

Baylor doesn't show his emotions very much at all. I know he doesn't like to sit out games. I know it by knowing the makeup of the guy. He wants to be out there every day. He wants to face every pitcher. He won't concede that any pitcher can get him out. But he doesn't want to rock the boat. He realizes we have an excess of talent and that the other guys have to get some playing time.

The game hasn't officially started until Baylor walks down the bench and yells at the opposing pitcher, "Get that weak shit over the plate." Every day in the first inning of the game you can hear Don and know the game has officially started. Otherwise he's very quiet. He doesn't force himself on people, doesn't say an awful lot. But he has tremendous confidence in himself as a batter. You can't hurt him. If he gets hit with a pitch, he never rubs it or says ouch. He drops his bat and walks to first base. And he's strong. The pitchers don't want him coming after them. He could body slam any pitcher in the league. I've seen him hit in the back, the shoulder, and the arm. It seems he gets hit in the bicep once a week. It never seems to bother him.

Baylor was accepted from the day he came over here. He has all-star credentials, MVP credentials, and now that he's started hitting home runs, I'm sure he's a lot happier. He's the kind of guy who says, "Leave me alone. Let me do my job, and check my numbers at the end of the year."

You cannot win a pennant with speed in Yankee Stadium. We proved that last year. In our park you have to have left-handed power, and Steve Kemp was supposed to provide that. As yet Kemp has not been a power hitter for us. He doesn't pull the ball much at all. He hits home runs to left center, center, and right center, and I think Yankee Stadium has probably hurt him more than helped him. He was better off in ballparks like Detroit or Chicago, where balls go out in left center and right center. I've seen him hit many balls 420 feet—they'd be home runs somewhere else, but here they only carry to the stadium's warning track. I don't think he'll ever hit more than twenty home runs a year in Yankee Stadium.

What I love about Steve as a player is that he can contribute in so many other ways. He's a good hitter with men on base. He fights the ball off. He can hit to left field. He plays so darn hard, I'm surprised he doesn't hurt himself more.

He was on first base with two outs when Baylor hit a popup that looked like it was going way foul into the left field stands. When the ball blew back and landed on the left field line, Kemp had scored all the way from first. Afterward he told me, "With two outs, I had nothing else to do, so I figured I might as well run." From our dugout, we could see the ball seven or eight rows into the stands, and then the wind brought it back, and it landed on the line as everyone stood around watching it. When the ball hit, Baylor was still standing on home plate. If they had thrown to first instead of throwing home to get Kemp, they would have gotten Baylor. It was that kind of popup. Fortunately, Kemp didn't have the angle Baylor had, and he couldn't tell whether it was fair or foul, so he ran. When the ball hit fair, no one could believe it.

Another time Kemp scored from second when I hit a sacrifice fly to left field. The left fielder crashed into the wall catching it, and Steve didn't stop until he crossed home plate. I got an RBI. I told him, "Thank you very much. Nice hustle." He's the kind of guy who runs over the catcher at the plate. He plays hard. He could play for me anytime.

We're winning a lot of games right now. We won eight in a row, but just are not able to make up any ground because everybody in the AL East is playing the other division, and everyone is beating up on the West. We won nine out of ten and gained one game on Baltimore and Toronto. Some people say this is unfortunate. I look at it as positive. If we hadn't won, we might have dropped another five games in the standings. We have to keep pace and hope we get hot when we start playing teams in our division again.

Baltimore is holding up, and Detroit, and Milwaukee is getting hot, and Toronto is playing well, and we're right up there. Every team is hot except Cleveland. It's going to be a six-team race. It's going to be wild, unless one team can get off on a real tear.

Football is always talking about parity, how on any given Sunday any team can beat another team, but somehow it's still Dallas or Miami in the Super Bowl all the time. Parity has come to baseball. In every division there are four teams within a couple games of first place. In the American League West, Kansas City is in fourth place, three games out. Texas, Chicago, and California are there too.

Normally I don't watch the standings until the middle of August, when the games begin to mean more. But this year I keep finding myself asking, "How did Toronto do last night?" I never thought I would ever care what Toronto did in the middle of July. "They won again? Oh, no." It's that kind of year. The thought hit me, "What if Toronto and Montreal made it to the World Series? Would they only play one national anthem? The Canadian anthem?" They'd say, "Screw 'The Star-Spangled Banner.' We don't have any American teams playing in this thing.'' 'Cause when we go up there, we always have to stand through those two national anthems, which is a royal pain in the ass, especially in the cold weather.

I don't know why the East is so much better than the West, but it's been that way ever since they began divisional play. It's been fourteen years. Look at the standings. Every team in the East is above five hundred except for Cleveland. And there's only one team in the West, Chicago, playing over five hundred. It's very strange. It shouldn't happen that way year after year, but it does. Maybe it's because the teams in the West have to do so much traveling. Every road trip for them is a major trip. A lot of our trips are an hour or two. Also it's easier to go from east to west and play than the other way. You gain three hours going out there. Coming back here you lose three hours.

It's mid-July, and the game for me is still fun because we're winning. The summer becomes a drag only when you're losing, like last year, when we were out of it early. I couldn't wait for the season to be over with. This year, though, it's different. We're only four games out of first, and even though we're struggling to find a combination that'll win for us, it's exciting. It's fun to go to the ballpark every day knowing you're in a pennant race. The fans don't understand this, but the amount of money you're making has nothing to do with whether the game is fun or not. The money and the game are separate. The fun has to do with how well the team is playing. If I was making a million a year and we were out of it, it would not be fun. And I'm not saying the money isn't important. I am saying that the fun is still more important than the money. The fun part of the day is being in the locker room with the twenty-five guys, or being out on the field.

The *Post*'s Mike McAlary gave all the players a grade, like we were school kids coming home with report cards. I got an A. Last year the *Post* gave me a D. I appreciate his opinion, but writeups don't win games. Last year Griffey probably got a D, and now he's at the head of the class with an A. It's humorous, unless you're down in the D's and F's. How can he give Matt Keough a D? Matt hasn't pitched badly. He has Bert Campaneris down as a C. To me he's an A. He's done everything they've asked of him. He's played all different positions, he's hitting .350. What more do you want at his age for a guy who last year was playing in Mexico?

Some of the guys get really mad when they see what's written about them in the papers. Willie Randolph sees red when he reads that he won't play hurt. He's tried to stop looking at the papers, but any time something is written, Oscar Gamble will come in and with a big grin tell him about it. "Did you see what they said about you today, Willie?" And sometimes, even when nothing is in the paper, Oscar will make it up just to piss Willie off.

Oscar is still waiting for the Yankees to trade Mumphrey, so he can get his house.

Oscar mangles words like Yogi does. The other day when Ray Fontenot pitched a good game, Oscar said, "It was a good deal when we got Footnote from Texas." He calls him Footnote. It's a good thing Oscar has a sense of humor. This has been a tough year for him. It's his option year, and he doesn't play much. But he hasn't complained about it.

I love the idea that there is always something crazy going on with the Yankees. As long as the craziness isn't directed at me. And it keeps the fans coming out to the ballpark. Look at the Mets. The only controversial player they have is Kingman, and he isn't even playing now.

People don't bother to come out unless there is controversy. George knows that. We'll have forty thousand people out to a nice Saturday evening game, whereas the Mets might have seventeen thousand. It's a lot more fun to play in front of forty thousand than in front of seventeen.

Because George pays his players such high salaries, the fans say to themselves, "There must be something special about these guys," and they pay their money to get in and see them play. Which is why I don't understand it when George knocks his players. You would think that when he says, "Winfield isn't worth a damn," or "Reggie isn't worth a damn," the fan would say, "Why would I pay money to see the star in the play when the producer says he isn't worth a damn?" I've never understood that about him. I can't see someone backing a Broadway play, and then after the first week saying, "This play stinks. The performers are rotten. But I want all of you to come out and see it." It's beyond me the way that man thinks.

One time I thought I was beginning to understand George. A few years ago he made a decision, and I said to myself, "I think I'm beginning to figure this guy out." Then I thought, "Aw no, I don't even want to be able to figure him out, because I don't want to ever think like he does."

It's hard to know exactly what's on George's mind as far as what he intends to do about a contract for me for next year. I could have signed a one-year extension, but I've decided to stick it out to the end and see if I can get more than a year from him. It helps to know that Billy doesn't like Smalley as a third baseman. I don't know how things will be at the end of the year, whether George will do it all on his own or whether he will take advice from Billy. I wish George would take Billy's wishes into account, because he's the one who sees us every day. He's the one who has to field the team. In the past George has gone out and gotten all the players, and then handed them to the manager and said, "Here, win with these guys." Why not let the manager tell him, "This is who we need; this is who we don't need"? If he takes Billy's advice, I can be here a few more years. But you never know. You never can get a reading on what George is going to do.

This is also the final year of Goose's contract, and Goose says he intends to become a free agent and go somewhere else. Goose says playing here isn't any fun. I wouldn't blame Goose for becoming a free agent. If George hasn't offered him a contract by now, if he can't see his value after five and a half years, Goose might as well wait a couple more months and play it out. The way Goose throws the ball, he could name his price.

Goose is pitching as hard this year as he ever was. That's what teams look for: whether his arm is sound. He's been getting beat, but he gives up runs on little dinky hitters.

Unfortunately for Goose, none of the middle relievers have been pitching very well. We have excellent starting pitchers, but we still need to find someone who can do what Ron Davis used to do for us. He would come in in the sixth or seventh, and he'd pitch two or three innings of shutout ball until Goose came in to finish up. When Davis was pitching for the Yankees, we never lost a game in which we were ahead. Unfortunately, George never understood his value, and he traded him away for a shortstop we didn't need. We haven't been the same team since. I can see getting rid of a guy when you have a glaring need at the position you trade him to fill, but at that time we had Bucky, who had done a great job for us. And Davis had done a great job for us. This is where George's emotions get the best of him. Davis took him to arbitration and won, so George was going to show him. George's way of letting you know you're in his doghouse is for him to threaten you by saying he's going to send you to Toronto or Minnesota. Now it might not be such a bad deal to get sent to Toronto. He's sent so many guys there that Toronto is in first place. Half that team are former Yankees.

There's talk of Goose going to the Mets, but if Goose

goes, he'll want to go to a team that wins. That lets the Mets out. People say the Mets are getting closer. Closer to what, fifth place? And when they do win, the only reason is that they have Jesse Orosco in the bullpen. So what's Goose going to do there? A team can only have one short reliever.

Goose and I have talked in jest about going as a package a la Drysdale and Koufax. It's not a bad idea. Maybe we will.

I don't have any idea where I'll go. Anyplace that wants me, I suppose. I'd like to stay here. I'm used to it after eleven years. I've been through a lot worse times than I've been through this year. I'd like to stay here, and I'd like to see Goose stay here too.

I want at least two years, and George has said he would only talk one year. That's not good enough. I just hope that when it comes down to it George consults Billy, 'cause Billy is on the field every day, and he sees who has what value to the ballclub. He knows that I'm a valuable player on the team, and maybe he could sway George's thinking. Whereas George might be thinking, "Finally here's my chance to get rid of Nettles, to get him out of my hair." I just hope Billy doesn't do anything silly and get fired before the year's out, because that would hurt my position.

When we were playing the Royals in Kansas City, I noticed that George Brett had too much pine tar on his bat. I was playing third, and I saw George getting ready to hit, and I saw him gripping his bat way up on the handle with the pine tar on his hands. Then I looked at the bat, and from where I was, I could see the pine tar way up past where it was supposed to be. At the end of the inning I came in and told Billy and Butch Wynegar, who was catching. I said, "If Brett gets a big hit in this series, let's ask to check his bat for too much pine tar." It had happened to us. It had been called on Thurman Munson back in 1975. Thurman got a base hit against Minnesota and drove in a run, and their manager came out, and the home plate umpire looked at the bat, took out a little tape measure, and showed that the tar was more than eighteen inches up the barrel, and called Thurman out and made the runners go back. Thurman was upset. He called the umpire everything in the book. But the umpire said, "Hey, this is the rule. The rule stands." So I remembered that. Since then, I conscientiously clean the pine tar off my bat when it's up too high.

I use pine tar. It gives me a better grip on the bat. Sometimes you touch the pine tar, and then you put your hand high on the bat, and if you do that enough times, a buildup of pine tar becomes visible. That's what Brett did. I told Billy, "If he gets a big hit, we'll call it to the attention of the umpires—afterward." But in Kansas City Brett didn't hurt us. And then early in the New York series, Brett broke the bat hitting against Fontenot. I thought, "Well, that's the end of that." I hadn't figured that his next bat would have even more pine tar on it. The next game he came up, and when he hit a home run in the top of the ninth against Goose, Rick Cerone remembered that he was to check Brett's bat, except that he didn't know what he was supposed to look for. Rick checked to see if it was corked, and when he saw it wasn't, he tossed it aside. But Billy came out of the dugout and said, "Wait a minute. Check the bat for pine tar." The Royals' bat boy had already grabbed the bat and started back to the dugout, but the umpire called him back, and the umpires looked at it. As they were doing so, I walked in toward home plate, and I saw the pine tar was a good eight to ten inches above where it was supposed to be. Billy said, "That's an illegal bat. The pine tar is too high. The rule says it can't be more than eighteen inches above the handle."

The umps didn't have a ruler, so they laid the bat across home plate, which is seventeen inches wide, and you could see the tar a good ten inches more, so they had no recourse but to call Brett out and nullify the home run. George Brett came running out of the dugout like a crazy person. I stayed on the field to try to calm George down. He looked like he was going to run right over an umpire or maybe take a swing at one. I mean, I can understand how upset he would be. I said, "George, don't do anything that will hurt you." I was yelling that at George, trying to calm him down. One of the umpires had hold of him, and that's when Rocky Colavito went up to the umpire who had the bat, and as he was talking to him, Gaylord Perry grabbed the bat out of the umpire's hand and started for the clubhouse. He wanted to get rid of the evidence. They started passing it between themselves, and finally the last guy in the row didn't have anyone to pass it to, and by then the umpire had caught up with the bat.

We won the game, and we won it legally. It may be a

chickenshit rule, but it's a rule. I saw us lose a hit and an RBI on the rule, so I figured the same rule is still on the books and applies to this situation.

After Brett got called out, we went into the clubhouse figuring we had a win. We knew he got caught with an illegal bat, and there was nothing they could do about it. We all teased Goose. I said, "Goose, you actually get a save out of that? You came in and gave up a home run and got a save?" He said, "I'll take them any way I can get them." It was like we beat them when we really didn't beat them. Strangest game I have ever played.

I once lost a hit on an illegal bat. A guy in Chicago who was a Yankee fan said, "Let me have one of your bats. I'll fix it up for you." He was a friend of Bill Sudakis, who was a catcher on our team. Everybody talks about what it's like to use a corked bat, and he said, "I'll fix up a corked bat for you." The ball is supposed to jump off the bat farther, but I couldn't really tell the difference when I used it one game. I did hit a home run with it, but the home run I hit would have been a home run even without it. But then the next time up, I connected, and the end of the bat came off. I felt like a fool. I saw the ball go one way and the end of the bat go another way.

There's a myth that little balls came flying out of the bat, but that never happened. Nothing came out. He had sawed an inch of the end of the bat off and then plugged it down the middle with cork, and then glued the top back on. He said it was great glue and that it would never come off. The glue came undone the second at bat I used it.

The umpire pointed at me and said, "You're out." For using an illegal bat. I knew that was a rule. If you get caught using an illegal bat, you are called out. A rule's a rule.

Four days after our win in the Pine-Tar Game, American League president Lee MacPhail made a mockery of the rule book. He declared that, while George Brett's bat was clearly illegal, it wasn't illegal enough for him to be called out. He ruled that the game should be continued from the point where Brett was called out. I didn't know that a rule could be interpreted as MacPhail said, for the "spirit of the rule." When we found out MacPhail overruled the umpires, I couldn't believe it. I think of it like our making a citizen's arrest. We see a guy jaywalking, and we tell a cop, "This man is jaywalking," and the cop says, "You're right. He is," and he gives him a ticket. When you go to court, you don't expect the judge to overrule the cop. But that's what MacPhail did. If MacPhail had been the judge, he would have told the cop, "Oh, hell, he wasn't trying to get hit by any cars." That's the way it looks to me. And what makes it worse is that in the past umpires had warned Brett that he had too much pine tar on his bat and had told him to stop doing it. Yet he ignored them and kept on doing it. It's a silly rule, and yet it's a rule, and we knew about it, and we caught him, and he should have been called out.

Billy was furious. The day after the game he was talking with George Sisler, who is on the rules committee, and when we were down in Texas, he talked with Bobby Bragan, who used to run the Texas League, and both of them told Billy that we couldn't lose. So we were very confident. And then we went to Chicago and found out we lost the decision. And when we heard that, we went out and lost five of the next six games. I don't want to use that as an excuse, even though other people might, but we had been playing well, we had our momentum, and whammo, MacPhail took that win away from us, and for the next week we played badly.

According to MacPhail's ruling, we're now supposed to play a four-out game that could end up determining the pennant. And he's going to make us play on August 18 in violation of the Players Association agreement against playing more than nineteen days in a row. We have to decide whether or not we're going to play if they say we have to.

In the next game against Chicago Billy really made an issue out of the rule book. That's the way Billy is when he feels he's been cheated. Billy is one sore loser. There was a play at home plate, and Cerone went to make the tag, and the runner was clearly out, and umpire Dan Morrison called him safe. Cerone went to argue, and as he did so he stumbled and ran right into Morrison. When Morrison felt the contact, he threw Cerone out of the game.

Billy went out to argue.

The night before umpire Dale Ford and Billy had had a run-in. Billy had said some bad things about him in the newspaper. When I went to home plate to deliver the lineups the next day Ford said, "Tell Billy I really appreciate the things he said about me in the papers." Real sarcastic. I said, "I didn't read the paper. What did he say?" Ford never gave me an answer.

After the Cerone incident happened at home plate, we had to bring another catcher in, Wynegar. Wynegar was warming up, and Ford said, "Okay, that's it, you've had five throws. That's all you can have." And here comes Billy out of the dugout saying, "There's nothing in the rule book that says if a catcher gets thrown out the new guy can only have five throws." And there is nothing in the rule book that says that. They went round and round and round, and it looked like he was about to throw Billy out. They were jawing back and forth, and Ken Kaiser, one of the other umpires, stepped between Billy and Ford, and he had Billy's shirt in one hand and Ford's shirt in the other. When Billy said the magic word, he started to throw Billy out of the game, but when he brought his arm up he ripped all the buttons off Ford's shirt. Ford was standing there with his shirt open all embarrassed. In the dugout we all started laughing. I went over to Billy, and I said, "How did that guy's shirt get ripped," and by then Billy was laughing, and he doesn't usually laugh after he gets thrown out of a game.

It was one of those Sunday afternoons in Chicago where just about anything can happen. Goose was telling me that he saw some of the strangest games in his life on Sunday afternoon in Chicago. That day we had eight critical calls in the game, and seven of them went against us. Some of them were really obvious. When things like that happen, Billy thinks people are ganging up on him.

BALLS

After the game, Billy redeclared war on the umpires. He called one of them a "stone liar," whatever that means. And now he's going to be suspended.

I could see it building in Billy from the first inning. It was a hot day. About a hundred degrees. I said to somebody on the bench, "Billy is going to get thrown out today." I could see it right from the opening, because he was upset from the pine tar ruling of the night before. I could see he was seething inside. And sure enough, around the fifth inning, Billy got the heave ho.

10

1978

When I arrived at spring training in 1978, I assumed things would continue to remain on the same crazy level, and I was certainly right. We had the fortune—or misfortune, depending on how you want to look at it—of winning with all the controversy, drawing more fans than ever before. So I knew the controversy was going to stay, at least until we started losing, which seemed to be the case in July of '78, when Billy got fired. Players seemed to be angry all year. Reggie was angry with Billy, and Thurman was angry with Reggie, and Willie and Roy White were angry about their contracts, and Bucky was angry because Billy was always pinch-hitting for him, and Sparky, Ed Figueroa, and Mickey Rivers were angry for different reasons.

Sparky's was a case of George going out and getting a guy because he was available, even though we didn't really need him. It's the same thing we did with Smalley. We had a shortstop, Bucky Dent, but Smalley became available, so George got him. Same with Goose. He was available, so George got him. Sparky had just won the

Cy Young Award, so it was just a case of stockpiling players. You can't do that and keep the players happy.

Figgy was a guy who always seemed to be mad about something. And toward the end, he didn't want to pitch for us. He was upset with George about his contract, like everyone else, but Figgy decided that if he wasn't going to get the money he wanted, he was going to punish George. Unfortunately, he was punishing us as well. He said, "I just don't care anymore," and he didn't. When it came time to award World Series shares at the end of the year, I voted to give him nothing.

Mickey was just Mickey. Whatever money he had, he had already spent it. So he needed money every day. Also, he was always getting in trouble with his wife. One time he didn't come home after a game in New York. He spent the night somewhere else, and the next day he pulled into the stadium parking lot in his Cadillac, and waiting for him in their little Mercedes SL was his wife, and right there in the parking lot they started playing demolition derby. Mickey was holding on to the steering wheel, and wham, she smashed the Mercedes into the Cadillac. His eyes were bugging out of his head as she was smashing up the cars. She hit him seven or eight times, knocked him a hundred feet across the parking lot. Then she went home and burned all his clothes. For a week he went around wearing Adidas sweatsuits.

Most of the squabbling was the direct result of the imbalance brought on by the money George gave to the free agents. During the winter after the 1977 season George paid millions to Goose Gossage, Andy Messersmith, and Rawly Eastwick, and the players who had made the club so good, Sparky, Roy, Willie, Thurman, resented the money Reggie and Goose and Gullett were getting. What George should have done was give them their money and then give everyone else a raise too. That would have been the right thing to do, but of course he didn't do it, and it made many of his veteran players resentful.

George also made me angry when he tried to keep me from going to the all-star game. I had been picked for the team, and about three days before the game I hurt my toe, and without consulting me, George decided to yank me from the roster. The game was being played in San Diego, my hometown, and without telling me, he just dropped me off the team. The game was scheduled for Tuesday, and I had hurt the toe the Friday before, but I certainly could have played.

The press got wind of it, and George looked kind of foolish, and on Monday I got a call at home in Southern California, where fortunately I was spending the break. "Reggie's sick, and they need another guy on the roster." I drove down and appeared in the game. I played the last inning. But it was as though George was trying to embarrass me by taking me out of an all-star game being played in my hometown. It was his way of trying to push me around. Why? Maybe because I had called him a "fat motherfucker" a few years before.

One of the events I remember vividly from '78 is Reggie's deliberately defying Billy by bunting when Billy ordered him not to. Dick Howser, the third-base coach, had walked down the line and told him, "The man wants you to hit away," and then Reggie came back to the plate and tried to sacrifice. It was hard to believe I was sitting in the dugout of a major league team. It was like Reggie was saying to Billy, "Fuck you." I don't know what was going through Reggie's mind when he did it. Maybe he saw it as a final test to see what Billy would do. And so Billy suspended him for five days, and during those five days we won all the games, and for the first time all year the clubhouse was peaceful. And the day Reggie came back, instead of going out and taking batting practice, he held a press conference in the clubhouse. And that's the thing that pissed Billy off the most. Billy felt that Reggie had been away for five days and was rusty, and he should have been out on the field before the game getting ready. All the players knew Reggie should have been out there, and perhaps somebody should have said something to him, but he was standing in the clubhouse in front of all those reporters, and something like that would have just made more headlines, so none of us did. I suppose it should have been Billy's job to tell him, but Billy has always been reluctant to confront people, so it didn't happen. It was after that game that Billy exploded, calling Reggie a born liar and George a convicted one.

The next morning I found out about the comment. We were in Kansas City, and as I was walking through the mall in the hotel, Billy called me aside. He said, "I'm calling a press conference at four o'clock this afternoon. I'm going to resign." I told him, "It's probably better for you that you do, the way things have been going." He told me he had had a test done and that he had a spot on his liver. I said, "It's probably better for you this way." I was almost relieved for Billy. He seemed close to having a nervous breakdown, and he had been acting a little strange—suspending Reggie and then calling Reggie and

George liars. I could see he was acting a little irrational. It was best he get away from the game and view it from a different perspective.

A few hours later he called his press conference. That night Dick Howser managed the team, and the next night we got to the ballpark and Bob Lemon was in the manager's office. And right after that, we got over our injuries, and we had a set lineup for the next two months, and we marched through the East and beat everybody. It was much quieter with Lem there. If anyone said anything about Lem, he'd let it roll off his back.

And then a few days later, on Old-Timers' Day, it was announced that Billy was coming back to manage in 1980. That's when I first came out with the line about how some kids dream of joining the circus and others dream of playing baseball, and that I was able to do both. George didn't like my referring to his team as a circus. Even though he was running it like a circus. I didn't think it was so bad, especially compared to the comment Billy had made a couple days before. The circus draws a lot of people and is fun to watch.

When we came to Old-Timers' Day, we were told there was going to be a special announcement. Who knew what? It could have been anything. The last thing I was thinking about was that Billy was going to be rehired. Normally Joe DiMaggio is the last old-timer announced, because he had to be last or he wouldn't show up, but this time they must have told him what was going on, because after DiMaggio, the PA announcer said, "And the new manager for 1980," and we were all sitting in the players' lounge watching the introductions, and here came Billy out of the dugout, and he ran out onto the field, and the people were screaming and yelling, and I said to myself, "What in the hell is going on here?" We looked at one another and kind of laughed. Except for Reggie, of course. But despite how bizarre it was, I really wasn't shocked. Every week there was something unusual that outdid the something from the week before. The strange had become common.

It was the perfect publicity stunt, orchestrated by the master, George. For the next nine months all the fans talked about whether Billy was really going to manage or not.

Lem accepted it. He's an old soldier, a company man. Whatever George wanted him to do was fine with him. Lem never got too excited about anything. And like everyone else George fired, he got a bonus. George told him to go out and have a good time on the West Coast, which is where he lives.

We finished the season in a tie with the Red Sox. We played our final regular-season game on Sunday, and we flew to Boston to play at Fenway Monday afternoon. There was no time for us to really get nervous about it.

A few things about that game stand out in my mind: Bucky Dent's three-run home run, obviously. Also, there was a play that Piniella made in right field that probably saved the game for us, because it kept the tying run from scoring. There was a line drive hit to him, and it was hit into the sun, and he reached out with his hand at the last minute and stabbed at it and kept the runner from going to third base. The next batter hit a fly ball that would have scored him had he gotten to third, and tied the game up.

People forget that Reggie hit a big home run. Everybody thinks that Bucky's home run off Mike Torrez won it, but actually it was Reggie's home run that put us ahead five to three, and they got a run later. So Reggie's home run was the winner in that game. A lot of people forget that, but it was one of the biggest clutch home runs he hit for us.

And I remember the final popup. Yaz came up. Against Goose. We were up by a run. The winning run was on base. I had seen Yaz do it before. When I was with the Twins in '67, he demolished us in the final two-game series and won the pennant. So I was hoping this was no déjà vu. I was thinking to myself, "Hey Yaz, how 'bout a popup right now," and on the first pitch he popped it up—to me. I suddenly thought, "Not to me. Please, not to me." I was staggering under it.

Luckily, it wasn't the towering kind that the wind could get hold of. It was a semi-popup, and I didn't have any trouble with it.

Winning the pennant after so much turmoil was fantastic. I didn't do anything offensively that game, but it was the greatest thrill just to be able to play.

We got right on the plane and went to Kansas City. We knew not to celebrate real hard because we had done that in '76, and we hadn't been in any shape to play the World Series. So the airplane flight was pretty much subdued. That's part of the experience of winning. We knew how to celebrate, whereas in '76 we were rookies at celebrating.

In the World Series the Dodgers won the first two games in their park. Guidry pitched the third game for us, and they kept hitting balls all around me, and I caught everything they hit, turned the game around, saved us a lot of runs. From there we took the next three games and took it all. It topped off the whole year. We came back in the pennant race, we came back in the game against Boston, we came back in the World Series.

After we won the World Series against the Dodgers in 1978, you would have thought George would leave the team alone, because it was a team that looked like it was going to win for a long, long time. Chambliss, Willie, Bucky, and I were in the infield, Thurman was catching, and we had Roy White, Mickey Rivers, and Reggie in the outfield. It was a set team. Leave it alone. Don't touch it. But during the winter Rod Carew announced he was going to be a free agent, that he wanted to get away from Calvin Griffith in Minnesota—which made perfect sense—and George announced that he was going after him. Bowie Kuhn had allowed Carew to negotiate with other teams, even though he was still owned by Minnesota. He said Carew could call around and make his own deal, which was normally against the rules. But that was Bowie's way of doing things. Different players get different treatment. And during negotiations, Carew finally decided he was going to California, that he wasn't going to play for the Yankees, and George told the press that Carew didn't appreciate the privilege of playing for the Yankees in New York. George is always talking about how he represents New York, how he gives his all for New York, except that he's from Cleveland, and he lives in Tampa.

The way George does things makes me laugh. He'll want someone and want him and want him, and then when the player decides he doesn't want the Yankees,

George'll bad-mouth him. He did that with Don Sutton, too. When Sutton was a free agent, George went after him hard, and finally when Sutton turned him down, he said, "Well, we really didn't need him in the first place." George has never learned how to lose. He thinks being a good loser is a sign of weakness. And that's not how life is. You're going to lose sometimes.

11

There doesn't seem to be much consistency on this Yankee team. Even though we're only a couple games out, it seems we should be five games ahead. Dave Winfield has been hitting the ball awfully well, has carried us for a couple of weeks. But when he doesn't hit, we don't seem to generate many runs. Our problem is that there are a lot more good teams than there used to be. We used to beat the White Sox ten out of twelve games a year. Now they're beating us. The teams are so evenly matched that it's hard to put distance between us and the rest of the pack.

Despite our struggling, George has been mercifully quiet. Of course, the vultures from the press did everything they could to put an end to that. After we lost five out of six to Chicago and Toronto, there was a headline in the *Post* that said tauntingly, "George Silent as Yankees Sink." The newspapers blast George when he pops off, and they blast him when he's silent. I mean, it's hard for me to sympathize with George, the way he's treated people, but you almost feel sorry for him in that sometimes he can't win for losing either. The reporters have become accustomed to him popping off every other day in the papers, and now that he's silent, they egg him on, call him up at home and ask him questions.

In Toronto there are sea gulls flying all over the stadium. I was standing near third base between innings, when a gull dive-bombed ten feet away from me, flew by the mound, and then flew out into right center field and landed. It tumbled around and then sat up. Something seemed wrong with the bird.

Dave Winfield was playing center field that day, and he was throwing with someone in the right field bullpen. On an impulse, he threw the ball at the bird, knowing that you never hit a bird when you throw a ball at it. The bird always gets out of the way. But this bird didn't move an inch. The ball took one hop, hit it right in the neck, and the sea gull dropped over dead.

About three pitches into the inning, I heard everybody yelling. Toronto called time out, and the bat boy ran out into center field and threw a towel over the body of the bird.

Later in the game Oscar Gamble hit a fly ball off the center field wall, and their center fielder, Barry Bonnell, went back to try to catch it, and two sea gulls were standing right on the warning track and slammed against his legs.

As the game ended, Billy said to me, "Do you know

what they're going to do?" I said, "What?" He said, "They're going to arrest Winfield." I said, "For what?" He said, "For killing that bird." "You got to be shitting me," I said. "Last inning I killed a moth. I hope they didn't see me killing that moth out there. If they revere sea gulls so highly, in what kind of esteem do they hold rats and cockroaches in Canada?" Hold a sea gull in esteem? Every fisherman and tourist in the world who ever got shit on by a sea gull would love to shake Dave's hand. What the hell good is a sea gull?

The gulls are a nuisance in Toronto. They're all over the field. I think Winfield should have been given a medal for killing the damn thing. I don't know one thing a sea gull is good for. You can go over to Shea Stadium and box up two or three hundred of them.

When the plainclothes cops burst into the clubhouse to arrest Dave, Billy was furious. He told reporters, "This is bush. I don't ever want to hear the Canadians knock us about the pine-tar business after this."

We went to the airport that night, and we had to sit an extra half hour waiting for Winfield. They took him right from the ballpark to the jail. He had to post a five-hundred-dollar bond before they let him out. He said he got to the jail, and they had the bird there wrapped in a towel. They interrogated him: "Did you kill this bird?" We said, "Dave, did you plead not *gull*ty?" He faces a cruelty-to-animals charge.

Ron Guidry, who knows all about hunting, said that Dave must have thought the bird was a laughing gull and figured that gull was laughing at him.

Billy said, "Yeah, but who got the last laugh?" He told the writers, "Maybe when the Blue Jays come to

New York next week, we should hold a memorial service for the bird. We can bury it back there by the monuments with the Babe.''

We went to Detroit after the Toronto series, and in the first game, when Winfield came to bat, all the fans in the center field bleachers stood up and started flapping their arms like sea gulls.

One day we came into the clubhouse, and someone had taped a stuffed bird above his locker. It looked like a real sea gull. He took it down.

A couple days later in the stadium two sparrows were out in the outfield right behind shortstop where Dave could have taken a throw at them if he wanted to. He smiled and just let the moment pass. He doesn't need the Audubon Society, the Environmental Protection Agency, the Sierra Club, or the Right to Lifers on his case.

Jerry Mumphrey was in Billy's doghouse much of July, but toward the end of the month Billy put him back in, and he has been playing excellently. He is one of the reasons the Yankees were so consistent toward the end of July.

Then comes the part I find hard to comprehend: once he begins playing well, they up and trade him, to Houston, for another center fielder, Omar Moreno. If that trade had taken place in the middle of June, nobody would have been surprised, because Mumphrey had asked to be traded, and he wasn't playing. But to do it when we are playing so well is a shock.

Before his last game here one of the writers came up to Jerry and told him that he was pretty sure he was going to be traded to Houston. Jerry went out and got a couple hits and made a great diving catch in the outfield. You have to admire a guy who knew it was his last game with the team and still went out and busted his butt. Some guys would have loafed through the game.

Before he left, I said, "Hope you enjoy where you're going." He's going back to Texas, which is his home. He's going back to the National League. I'm sure he's happy with the deal.

I can't say the same for Billy. Billy isn't high on a lot of National League players. He's an American League guy all the way. Moreno might have had one strike on him from the start, coming over from the National League.

The Yankees tried to trade Rick Cerone to Cincinnati for Bruce Berenyi and Alex Treviño. Rick turned it down. I don't blame him for not wanting to go to Cincinnati. That organization has been shabbily run for the last four or five years. I don't see why anyone in his right mind would okay a trade to go over there. They're in last place in their division, and we're almost in first. At this time of year it wouldn't make any sense.

It has always surprised me that the Yankees keep trading for guys from second-division teams. George gets these guys, and then he expects them to come over here and be immediate winners. It doesn't work that way. You have to have some experience on a winning club before you're going to win. If he wanted immediate winners, it would make a lot more sense for him to start trading with some first-division clubs, to get players who have been through pennant races before.

Every once in a while I have one of those days to write home about, and against Toronto at the stadium, I had one of those days. In the sixth there was a runner on first, and one of the Blue Jay hitters hit a hard liner down the third-base line. I made a desperate dive, backhanded the ball with my gloved hand stretched as far as I could possibly go, jumped back up, and made the forceout at second to kill a rally. I made four or five plays in that game, just caught everything hit my way. By the ninth inning I was so tired, a guy hit me a ball, and I dove and backhanded it, and trying to get up I stumbled, and I ended up sitting on the ball. I looked like I was trying to hatch an egg. My legs weren't under me when they should have been. I was worn out. I laughed, because by then we were so far ahead it didn't matter.

It was a very satisfying game. There was a nice crowd and it was very gratifying to make a lot of good plays in front of those people. Making a good defensive play means a lot to me, even more than hitting a home run, especially since last year people thought I had slipped so badly as a fielder that I was through. Plus when I was traded from Minnesota to Cleveland, the Cleveland front office was told, "You're getting a pretty good hitter, but this guy can't play a position." I worked at playing third base, and I've played it well, and I am proud of what I have done at third.

Brooks Robinson has been the best third baseman over the last fifteen years, but I've been right behind him. In the American League, for consistently good offense and defense, I would put myself and Buddy Bell right there. A couple of writers are pushing me as a Hall of Fame player. I don't worry about the Hall of Fame. Maybe I'll think about it after my career is over. But that would be quite a tribute.

At bat I seem to be back in the rut I was in earlier in the year. Every game I hit four balls hard, and they are all caught.

I had one productive game. I went four for five against the Angels, with a lot of luck. I got a couple of bloops, a check swing over third, and a weak ground ball up the middle. I hit the ball best on the out I made, a line drive to right field.

When I go four for five, there has to be some luck involved, because I will never get many infield hits, because I don't have the speed. To get four hits in a game, I usually have to hit the ball hard every time, and against major league pitching, that is difficult to do.

After the game I told a reporter that I had been watching the White Sox and taking notes, because they were beating us with bloop hits that were unbelievable. They beat Goose one game in extra innings with three straight bloops.

We were playing the White Sox, and they have a kid named Scott Fletcher at shortstop. The other night he popped up, and as he did, he threw his bat down and said,

"Dadgummit." I came right off the bench and started yelling at him. I said, "Come on, kid, this is the big leagues. You're allowed to say 'motherfucker.' You don't have to say 'dadgummit.' " I found out that Fletcher's one of those born-again Christians who won't swear. For the next couple of games, every time he would foul the ball off and miss, I'd yell, "Dadgummit."

It's always infuriating to play the White Sox, because Pudge Fisk calls the slowest games I've ever played in. He takes forever—no matter what he's doing. It's a tossup between him and Mike Hargrove as to who is the slowest player. They take so much time doing everything. When Hargrove is hitting, he goes through a routine, pulling on his uniform, stretching, waving to the crowd, tying his shoes—Alan Bannister of the Indians named him the MBP, the Most Boring Player. Fisk is right up there with him.

One night Righetti lost the game because Dave Phillips, who is a good umpire, called a balk on Righetti before Fisk, the batter, got into the batter's box. A balk is impossible unless the batter is in the box.

Phillips was watching Righetti. He should have been watching Fisk, who takes about twenty minutes to get into the batter's box. He saw Righetti make a balk move, but he didn't see that Fisk wasn't yet in the box. And because of that, we lost.

Whenever we play Chicago the game takes three to four hours, mostly because of Fisk. We played a one to nothing game that took well over three hours. Between Fisk and White Sox pitcher Britt Burns, who is another of the slowest workers I have ever seen, you can pull your hair out waiting for the ball to be pitched. I don't know why they do that. That's why I enjoyed playing behind Catfish or Jim Kaat or Guidry. They work fast. Fisk catches the ball, and he'll hold it for two minutes, and finally he'll throw it back, and then he'll arrange himself behind the plate, and then he'll give a signal. I don't know his wife, but I can't help thinking he sure doesn't seem to want to get home to see her.

The next night the Chicago pitcher was balking, and our third-base coach, Don Zimmer, complained about it and got thrown out of the game. He was yelling, "The guy is balking the same way Righetti did the night before." The umpire said, "No, the batter wasn't in the batter's box." Zimmer said, "The guy last night wasn't ready to hit in the batter's box either." The umpire, a rookie, turned to Zimmer and said, "Well, who in the hell are you to be telling me?" The guy had never heard of Zim! Zim, who's been in the majors since the early fifties, exploded. "Who in the hell am I?" he screamed. "Get some time in the league and you'll find out who I am, you bush cocksucker."

Nobody could figure out why Zim was thrown out of the game.

All of us are really furious with American League President Lee MacPhail. When the umpires called Brett out for hitting with an illegal bat last month, they were obeying the rules in the rule book. Brett should have been out, and the game over. But then MacPhail comes and says that no, Brett isn't out, his home run counts, and that the game has to be resumed from that point with two outs in the top of the ninth on August 18—a clear violation of our rules about playing no more than nineteen days in a row. That's two bad decisions right there.

George, who didn't like it any more than we did, decided to make the best of a bad situation, play the game at two o'clock and turn it into a fun day for everybody. Camp kids could come at two o'clock and have a picnic and see the four outs for only $2.50.

And then MacPhail made another ruling, that we had to play the game at six o'clock, ruining all of George's plans and probably ruining us as well. Six in the evening is absolutely the worst possible time to play. The batters can't see the ball because the shadows are so bad.

George complained: "Once again Lee MacPhail has favored the culprit. He's bending over backward to accommodate the guys who perpetrated the crime. The kids are being penalized to accommodate the Kansas City team." For sure George is going to get himself in hot water by saying what he's saying, but we certainly appreciate his sticking up for us. I can't understand MacPhail's rulings either.

We can't quite figure out how the end of this game is going to work. There are a bunch of guys who played in that game who are now on the disabled list. We've got guys on the team now who weren't on the team then. Can we use them, or do we have to use the other guys? Do we bring Mumphrey back from Houston for the remainder of the game? Campaneris was in that game. Can we use him even though he's on the disabled list? It opens up a whole can of worms. I hope it rains. Then MacPhail'll be in a hell of a mess.

We held a meeting and voted as to whether we wanted to play the last four outs of the Pine-Tar Game, and we all voted to not even play the game. To not show up. To forfeit.

We considered doing a lot of things. We talked about working out, and then once game time came, showering and going home. That way we would make Kansas City go to the expense of flying into town, and let Lee Mac-Phail worry about it. We decided not to do that, arguing that we wanted the off day. To play four outs, you still have to go to the park, put the uniform on, get up for the game. So we decided, the hell with it, we'll just stay home and forfeit. And that's the way it stood when we left that meeting the day before the scheduled date.

* * *

I still wasn't sure the guys would go through with it. Players kept asking, "What are we going to do about Thursday?" Billy was all for forfeiting the game, and George said he would back us a hundred percent, but we didn't have it in writing from George. We wanted it in writing before we went ahead on his word. And we didn't want to make a premature announcement, because then if it rained all day, we wouldn't have to forfeit because the game couldn't be played anyway.

Once Pine-Tar Day was at hand, I really didn't know what we were going to do. I didn't think it should have been left up to the players to decide. It was management's decision. George had told a reporter that it didn't make any sense to forfeit, 'cause we could have ended up losing the pennant by one game, when it was conceivable we could win. Which did seem very possible. All we had to do was score two runs. I decided I would just as soon play. I didn't have any special plans, though it was our last off day at home for the rest of the season. It created a hardship for some guys, ruined the day for doing anything else.

There was another aspect to the game that caused me to want to play. Our first hitter scheduled to be up, Don Mattingly, had hit in twelve games before the Pine-Tar Game, and twelve after, and in his first three at bats in that game, he didn't get a hit. If he were to get a hit, he would have a twenty-five-game hitting streak, the most in the majors, and a record for rookies. I wanted to play the game just to give him the chance to get the record.

But we don't know. We'll see tomorrow.

The night before the game George came and talked to us in the clubhouse and said, "I don't think you guys have much to worry about. The judge is going to put a stop to this game, so just concentrate on playing tonight, and don't worry about tomorrow's so-called Pine-Tar Game."

Then we went out and got beat by the White Sox. His speech didn't do too much good. He kept saying, "Put the game out of your mind," but we had talked about it for forty-five minutes right before we took the field against the White Sox. We kept saying, "Forget about it," and we kept talking about it. I can't forget about something when I'm talking about it. And there was more discussion about whether we should forfeit.

Finally I stood up and said, "I don't see how we can possibly forfeit." A lot of guys were saying that it would take a lot out of us mentally just to come and get dressed for the game and bla bla bla. But there are guys making a million dollars a year, and I couldn't see how it would take too much out of them to come and get dressed for just four outs. If we were four runs down, the possibility of winning would be remote. But we had a good chance of scoring a run, so I felt as captain it was my place to speak up and say that we should play. How would we be able to explain to our fans later, in September, if we ended up one game out?

At 10:30 the morning of the scheduled completion of the Pine-Tar Game, they told us the judge had made a ruling canceling the game. But then the American League appealed it, and this time the judge ruled against us, and they told us to be at the park at four o'clock regardless 'cause Lee MacPhail would forfeit it if we didn't have the players ready. We went to the park at four still not knowing whether we would play.

When we got to the ballpark, we were told the game was on. When Billy found out he was upset. He was upset the whole afternoon.

The press in New York played the Pine-Tar Game up big. They made it like it was going to be a historic event. And then nothing happened. None of the fans showed up. Apparently most people thought the game had been canceled, because there were only about two hundred people in the park. It was a strange feeling. I didn't walk out onto the field until five minutes before the game was to resume. I didn't know what to expect, whether there would be thirty thousand people or thirty. It was quiet in the big ballpark and everything was over in ten minutes.

Brett had hit the home run with two outs in the top of the ninth, giving Kansas City the one-run lead, and we retired their first batter, and then it was our turn. We made three quick outs and walked in. That was the strangest feeling of all. "Was that all there is to it?"

It was a farce, and worse, it was a loss, but I'm glad we showed up to play. It would have looked terrible if we had forfeited the game.

The night before the Four-Out Game I went to sleep around two, and around ten in the morning my kids woke me out of a deep sleep, babbling something about Andre Robertson getting hurt in a car accident.

The accident happened at five-thirty in the morning. Everybody immediately assumed, "He was drunk," but Andre doesn't drink. A girl who Andre had known from Texas was visiting him, and it was her first time in New York City, and he was going to take her on a Circle Line boat ride around Manhattan.

They had been in the city, and they went back to his home in Fort Lee, New Jersey, to get his camera before the first boat left at six in the morning. It had been raining lightly, and the West Side Highway was slippery, and on the way back to Manhattan he was driving along one of the worst stretches of road in the country, and he failed to negotiate a curve. The car went out of control, flipped over a couple times, and both Andre and the girl were thrown out.

When I got to the park for the rest of the Four-Out Game, everyone wanted to know about Andre. Nobody had been allowed to see him. Gene Monahan had gone to the hospital, and all he saw were Andre's clothes, and he said they were all torn up. Monahan said that Andre must have hit the pavement and skidded a long way. We were all expecting the worst.

After the Four-Out Game, we dressed and left quickly. We had arranged a party at Goose's house that night, and rather than hang around the clubhouse and feel angry, we got the hell out of there.

It was the first time in about five years that we had held a team party, our last chance to have a party for the year, because in September there are few off days and a lot of the families go home. We swam in Goose's pool, but there wasn't very much gaiety. We knew Andre was in trouble, and we were feeling too upset to enjoy ourselves very much.

Willie Randolph had picked up Andre's parents at the airport and taken them to see Andre. Willie said that Andre doesn't look too good. He said his neck had swollen up to about twice the normal size and that he was really cut up around his face and arms. Roosevelt Hospital said he doesn't have any broken bones, which seems miraculous.

The strangest part of the evening happened when I was playing volleyball in Goose's pool. I was sitting on a little rubber seat, and when I fell off, I was thrashing around at the deep end. I really thought I was going to hurt my shoulder, but I woke up the next day and made a throwing motion, and for the first time in weeks, I had no pain at all.

Despite all our troubles, we're still only two and a half games behind Baltimore, in fifth place, and there is no lack of enthusiasm.

Last year when we fell apart, we were out of it by August, so the rest of the year was merely playing out the season and trying to fatten up the average. Right now, we're still in the thick of it, and it's been no trouble at all to get up for the games. Every game is still an exciting experience. We have Oakland and Seattle and the Angels coming up, and those teams have not been playing well, and those are the teams you especially look forward to playing. I love to come to the ballpark and beat up on the teams that aren't playing good ball.

Everyone is still doing a lot of scoreboard watching, which is an encouraging sign, because it's a strong indication that everyone's thinking about the race, thinking of where we are in the standings. If only we could put together a seven- or eight-game winning streak. All year we've been hot and cold. There's been no consistency. Right now, that's all we need.

We're a team that has never gotten set. We've had some injuries to key players, and that's hurt us, and then when those players come back, we find ourselves with the same old problem: too many front-line players to satisfy. It's impossible to play a set lineup. Half the players don't know whether they are going to be playing the next day or not, but I can't worry too much about the other guys. I worry enough about myself being in the lineup every day.

I can't wait until we start playing the teams in our division again. Some nights, I look at the scoreboard, and every other team in the East has also won, and we don't gain any ground.

Surprisingly, despite not getting any productivity out of our right-handed pitching, we can still win the whole thing. The left-handers are carrying us. The last month Baylor and Winfield have been carrying us, but recently Winfield has been in a terrible slump. He's been jumping at the ball, jumping right off his feet and swinging. He wants to lead the league in home runs, and instead of swinging naturally, he is overswinging, trying for the home runs.

No, we haven't lost any confidence. We're right there. A couple of good wins would get us going.

I've tried to get Goose to throw his slider more than he does, but he won't listen to me. The ping hitters have been beating him because they've been hitting his fastball off the end of the bat. If he'd throw a few more sliders, they wouldn't make contact at all. He has a good slider. It's the old theory: You don't want to get beat on your second-best pitch. Therefore, in the tight situation, he'll rely on his fastball. If he threw a few more breaking balls, he would be better off.

Goose has been the focus of much attention, because every time Billy needs a relief pitcher in a tight spot, he calls Goose. You have to call Goose. You figure his bad luck is going to change. The only time he's been hit hard in a loss was when George Brett hit a home run to beat him, and in another game when John Lowenstein of the Orioles hit a home run to beat him. It's hard to fault a guy with a ninety-seven-mile-an-hour fastball, but he's in a can't-win situation. If he does throw the breaking ball, everyone is going to say, "Why didn't you throw your best pitch?" If guys hit that ninety-seven-mile-an-hour fastball, and in the major leagues they can, everyone says, "Why didn't you throw the breaking ball?"

He'll throw an inside burner, and the batter will break his bat and flair one over the infield. We don't hold it against him. He makes the pitch he wants to make, and then something like that happens, and we can only shake our heads.

And then you read the papers the next day, and the writers are just blasting him.

I can tell when Goose is furious with himself. I can see the look of exasperation in his face. He knows we don't hold it against him, but he feels he's let us down. He knows he's supposed to come in and save the game. He expects to do it. And he hasn't been.

We were tied nothing to nothing against Geoff Zahn of California in the ninth, and Goose came in for Righetti and gave up a run. Goose was heartbroken, because it was another one of those bloop hits. Fortunately, Willie hit a ball up the middle, it took a bad hop, and Grich couldn't handle it, and then Griffey got a base hit to win the game, so we went from a loss to a win just like that.

We joke with Goose, call him the Vulture, which was what they used to call Dodger relief pitcher Phil Regan. Regan used to come in with a lead, give up a run, and then get the win himself, which is what has been happening to Goose. But then the newspapers took it one step further and began calling him a Turkey, just to make him look bad. Goose is an emotional enough guy without his having to read that garbage. He gets extremely upset when he comes in and gives up a run or if he's hit hard. Bloop hits he knows are not his fault. He's done his job. It's the same thing with a hitter who goes up there and hits a wicked line drive at the second baseman. The batter's done his job. You've tried to hit the ball hard, and you've succeeded. Only it went right at someone. Goose is making good pitches, and the little ping hitters are beating him. He may not be striking out as many batters as he used to, but from where I stand I can see that he's throwing the ball just as hard. If he started resorting to breaking pitches and changeups, I'd start to worry, but there is absolutely nothing wrong with his fastball.

A lot of people felt bad for Righetti because he pitched so well and didn't get the win. I said, "Look at it this way. If he hadn't pitched so well, we wouldn't have gotten the win." That's the only important thing, that the Yankees win. As a player, I don't care which pitcher gets the win. That we get it is all that counts.

Then we played Oakland and got swept.

In the opener, we lost in fourteen innings, Goose walked a couple of batters, gave up a bloop, and then walked Rickey Henderson, and it cost us the game.

Goose has had a tough year, even though he has not been hit hard. The one disagreement I have with Billy is that Billy waits a batter or two too long before bringing him in. He should bring him in and allow him to give up a hit that won't cause a run. That's what Ralph Houk did with Sparky when Sparky was having his good year. He would bring him in a batter or two early, before he had to get that out. If Billy would do that, or let Goose start the inning, rather than bring him in with a man on second all the time, Goose would be a lot better off.

Maybe Billy got a little absent-minded about his bullpen when he was managing Oakland, 'cause he didn't have any bullpen. It seems that Billy goes with his starters for so long that Goose is forced to come in in a get-the-batter-out-or-else situation.

I never said that to Billy. It's not my place. We have pitching coaches who decide that. Except that Billy doesn't listen to his pitching coaches because he doesn't trust them.

Goose is playing out his option year. Maybe that has something to do with it. If I were a scout in the stands, he'd certainly be the number-one priority for my ball-club.

Usually, Goose will have a stretch of bad luck that runs a couple of days, sometimes a couple of weeks. This year it's a couple of months. For him, with his arm, to only have thirteen saves at this time of year isn't normal. It's been a bad-luck year for him, and it's got to change. We're hoping September will bring that change. Every time he comes into the game I'm confident, because I know how well he's throwing. I say to myself, "Tonight's the night." But that night hasn't come yet. They just keep blooping them in.

It's very frustrating to lose to a team like Oakland. We don't often get the box scores of the teams on the West Coast, and so here are guys, some of whom I've never even heard of, beating us, and it's frustrating.

Oakland has all these pitchers I never heard of. Heinemeuler, Atherton, Mike Warren. I kept thinking it was like Butch Cassidy and the Sundance Kid when they were being chased: "Who are these guys?" I never heard of any of them. Every time I looked up, there was another one. And they were beating us, and Oakland was one of the teams we were supposed to beat.

I don't know why the Yankees are losing right now. We've been so hot and cold. We sweep a good team like California, and then we get swept by a team like Oakland. It doesn't make any sense to me.

During that fourteen-inning loss, Oakland scored a cheap run when the umpires called Ray Fontenot for playing with his mustache. He was standing on the rubber, and he went to pick at his mustache, and the umpire said, "You're going to your mouth." It cost him a ball. And it ended up hurting him. It changed the count drastically. It was a stupid call by the umpire.

The next day, I was joking about it. I said, "All you guys are going to have to shave off your mustaches once George finds out about this." And sure enough, George told Fontenot to shave off his mustache. So silly. Ray didn't shave it off. Billy told him not to worry about it.

After the fourteen-inning game, everybody was kind of wasted. To lose it was a shame, and the next day everyone was kind of dead. That night I felt as bad as I've ever felt in a night game following a night game. And we got beat again, by Butch, Sundance, and their gang.

Our biggest problem has been our fourth and fifth starters. I doubt that our right-handed pitchers have won more than a handful of games. Billy got Keough over here from Oakland, but after a good start, Matt hasn't been able to throw strikes, and he's been getting knocked out early.

I was in the trainer's room, and I asked Monahan, "Who's throwing for us tonight?" He said, "Keough and Shirley." I said, "Huh?" He said, "Keough and Shirley." I said, "You mean Shirley's pitching in middle relief?" He said, "No," but he never explained it.

Before the game, Keough and Shirley were warming up together in the bullpen, and when it started, there was Shirley still warming up. I thought it strange, because Billy usually tries to build the confidence of players who are his favorites, and Keough has always been one of them. Billy convinced George to get Keough from Oakland, but it sure looks like he's changed his mind about him.

Keough has not been pitching well at all, and last night he walked the first batter, Henderson, who is leading the league in walks. Our pitching coach came right out to the mound to talk to him. The next batter flew out deep to center. Henderson stole second, and then the next batter hit a ball up the middle about three feet from Smalley's glove, and boom, Billy yanked Keough out of there. It was the quickest hook I've ever seen. Shirley came in and finished up.

When Billy came out to pull Matt, I was thinking of going out to the mound, but Billy didn't look in too good a mood, so I didn't. I was afraid Keough might say something, even though he's normally an even-tempered guy, and I didn't want to be there if they were going to get into a big argument on the mound.

By Keough's reaction, though, it looked like he knew that if he didn't start strong, he'd be gone. Instead of going to the clubhouse, he just sat down in the dugout and watched the rest of the game. There's been a lot of talk in the papers about our getting another pitcher for the stretch drive, and I'm sure he knows he's been the reason for all the talk. I've heard talk that we're angling to get Bob Welch, or Len Barker, or John Montefusco, or Mike Torrez. We need a right-hander who can win some games for us. So far we haven't found the guy. Jay Howell, who looked so good in the spring, hurt his knee and had arthroscopic surgery. To take his place, we called up Dave LaRoche. He was playing softball in his hometown in Kansas, and they signed him and sent him to Columbus, where he pitched three innings, and then they called him up. He sat on our bench for ten days, and when he came in, he got bombed.

It's so strange the way things work around here. Wouldn't it have been better to promote one of the kid pitchers from Columbus? It's the end of August, and Billy is still looking for a combination out of the bullpen that will come in and stop a rally. There has been no consistency. So he continues letting the starters go as far as they absolutely can, just so he doesn't have to dip into the bullpen.

After losing to Oakland, we beat Seattle on a home run by Omar Moreno, which was quite a surprise. Omar is a slap hitter, hits a lot of singles, triples if they get between the outfielders. Omar has been with the club a month, and I haven't heard him say three words. I don't kid with him, because it's hard to kid with someone who doesn't talk. You never hear him. I don't even know what his voice sounds like. If he was in the next room, and I heard his voice, I wouldn't know who it was. I have no idea whether he feels accepted on this team or feels like a stranger. Five years ago we had a clubhouse full of loud characters, but they've been replaced, which has taken a lot of the fun and color away. There are a lot of guys making a lot of money who don't say very much. Perhaps they talk to their bankers, but they sure don't say much around the clubhouse.

I don't imagine Omar likes his role here. He has a funny contract where he gets a base salary plus a bonus for every time at bat. He's hitting seventh and eighth in our lineup, and sometimes he doesn't play, so I don't imagine he's too happy about the whole situation. But he never says anything, so I don't know.

A clause like that puts a manager at a disadvantage right from the start. It was in the contract Moreno signed over in Houston. It's no wonder he was complaining about being platooned there. Every time he didn't play it cost him money. Over here, they've lost confidence in his hitting completely, and he's just going to be used for late-inning defense. It's going to cost him even more money.

There's been a lot of talk in the newspapers about the trade we made, Jerry Mumphrey to Houston for Omar Moreno. The press and the fans are on Omar, because he isn't hitting. Ballplayers don't judge other ballplayers as quickly as the fans do. We know it takes a while for a new player to become settled. The fans go hot and cold on him from at bat to at bat. Maybe if he ran a little more when he got on base, showed them what he can do, it would take the pressure off him. We aren't winning right now, and it seems that he is being singled out.

Moreno was messed up in his first game when he joined us in Detroit. On his first at bat the count went to three and oh, and the pitcher threw him a changeup. They don't do that in the National League. It blew his mind! It's going to take him a while to adjust.

Omar has the speed. In one game he hit a ground ball to first base and beat the pitcher to the bag by two steps. He has more speed than Mumphrey, and he can go get them in the outfield. That's what we need, a guy who can really get them. He's as fast as any center fielder in baseball. The big question is whether Moreno can hit left-handed pitching, because we see so much of it.

Omar is also at a disadvantage because Mumphrey was

playing very good ball and Billy wasn't at all happy with the trade. Billy had told them not to do it. Mumphrey was starting to play well again, and Billy was convinced Jerry was his everyday center fielder. Then they traded him.

And ever since we got Moreno, Mattingly hasn't been playing much. Moreno came over at the time Griffey came back, and it's just the same old problem. Too many players. Not enough positions.

They may have thought Moreno would do things here he couldn't do over there, but he has had a lot of trouble adjusting to the breaking ball in the American League. For a contact, slap hitter, he sure strikes out a lot. Who wants a slap hitter who strikes out a lot? Maybe George got him so we'd have the only one around.

Goose couldn't hold the Angels in the bottom of the ninth, and we lost again. Roy made two errors on the final play. He bobbled the ball and then threw it away, allowing the winning run to score. That was a bad game for Roy. It's a bad infield, and he said he always had problems on it. Some places it's hard as a street, other places it's soft like sand, so it's hard to get a true hop.

I can sympathize with the guy. I know what he's going through. The same thing has happened to me, and it can happen again to me. When you boot balls that cost you the ballgame, you feel very bad.

After the game, a reporter asked Billy if it was a tough

loss, and Billy said, "It's been tough since August 18," which was when Andre got hurt. Billy realizes the importance of a good-fielding shortstop. He feels Andre's loss a great deal. Billy wants George to bring up the kid from Columbus again, Bobby Meacham, to play short. Roy is really more of an offensive player. He spends a lot of his time thinking about hitting. Though he works on his defense, hitting is what's on his mind most.

Roy's a sensitive guy, but you have to have a hard shell playing here. If the press gets to you in New York, you're not going to last very long. They write good things and bad things. You have to learn to accept it.

Roy realizes that he's not the shortstop Andre is. The other night, when he had a bad game, booted some balls, he said to reporters, "What am I supposed to do? Billy writes my name in the lineup, and I go out there and play the best I can. I know I'm not the shortstop Andre is, but I give all I can." He doesn't get down on himself. Roy has filled in at third, short, and first, and he's gotten his share of hits, and even though he hasn't played as much as he would have liked, he has never complained. Roy is a professional.

We're losing games, and whenever that happens, the New York writers find it necessary to find a scapegoat, and right now that scapegoat is Roy. Andre isn't in there, and they are looking for someone to blame.

The other night we had a couple of guys thrown out at the plate. Zimmer came in after the second one and said, "Aw hell, I'm just trying to take some of the pressure off

Roy.'' Zim's good like that. He has a good sense of humor. He knows he screwed up, and he admits it. Other guys would put the knock on the base runner. Zim said, ''I'm trying to get the boo birds off Roy.''

There isn't much humor left, largely because of Andre, who cracked the vertebrae in his neck. Fortunately, his neck didn't snap, so he won't be paralyzed.

The toughest part is the girl. Andre keeps asking, ''How's the girl? How's the girl?'' They wouldn't tell him. At first they thought she was going to die. She broke her neck and she's going to be paralyzed from the waist down. They waited several days before they told him. It's going to take him a long time to get over this.

It's hard to make jokes when your teammate is in the hospital in bad shape. Some stuff still goes on. When Oscar was told he was batting fifth, he said, ''I guess that's better than hitting twelfth, where I have been playing.'' Oscar rarely gets to play now. Oscar was razzing Lou. ''When you come up, the left fielder takes a cigarette break. You can't pull the ball anymore. They're going to pull the old Satchel Paige routine on you. Pull all the outfielders in and sit them around the mound.'' Lou just scowled at him.

The Orioles have won eight in a row, the gap between us is widening, and Billy has become very sharp and moody. Billy hates to lose, probably more so even than George. George had been pressuring Billy to play Omar, but Billy met with George about Moreno in center field, and they took him out. I guess Winfield is going to be playing center. Or maybe Winfield against left-handers, Moreno against righties. It's too bad. If we hadn't traded Mumphrey, and if Andre hadn't gotten hurt in the car accident, there would be no way we'd be seven games back.

12

1979–1982

Bob Lemon had taken over as manager midway through 1978, and in June of '79, George fired him. Lem had lost his desire. Over the winter his youngest son was killed in a car accident, and Lem kind of went into a shell. He was a quiet guy to begin with, and he became even more silent and distant. He didn't seem to have his heart in the managing job anymore, so I think it was best for everybody that he get away from it for a while. So George brought Billy back for his second tour of duty. We knew George was going to bring him back eventually, and it made sense to do it when he did.

When Billy came back he was furious that George had traded away Dick Tidrow. Goose and Cliff Johnson had gotten into a fight in the clubhouse. It started out as a playful thing. People were throwing stuff around, like they always do, and some words were exchanged, and then Cliff and Goose began playfully shoving each other, and somebody shoved too hard, and then they started fighting. Goose tore his thumb up and wasn't able to pitch for a long while.

Tidrow had been pitching long relief, but when Goose got hurt, Lem threw him in as the short man, just like that. And Tidrow wasn't ready. For about a week he got hit real hard, and finally George got real impatient and said, "Get rid of him. Get him out of my sight," and Al Rosen traded him to the Cubs for Ray Burris. Billy felt that if he had been there the trade never would have been made, and Billy dumped on Burris and wouldn't pitch him much at all. Later that season Cliff was laughing on the bus after a loss, and George found out about it, and traded him off the next day. When you play for George, you come to live with the fact that he's going to make decisions based on emotion, not on a businesslike basis. Some of his decisions are good. Some are bad. The only time it takes him forever to make a decision is when you want something from him. Like more money.

Our season went up in flames on August 2, when Thurman was killed as he practiced takeoffs and landings in his new jet. About a week before the plane crashed, Reggie, Thurman, and I were flying in his plane from Seattle to Anaheim. Reggie and I were in the back, and his instructor was in the pilot's seat next to Thurman. Thurman had bought the Cessna just two weeks earlier, and the instructor was accompanying him on the road trip. We had just finished a night game in Seattle, and we were flying south, and all of a sudden I heard a big boom in the back of the plane. It sounded like someone had thrown something against the plane. Reggie was napping, and he jerked awake and looked around. "What was that?" he said, as the oxygen masks were dropping down. The pilot said, "You're going to have to use the oxygen." My mask worked, and Reggie's didn't. I told

Reggie, "Thurman told me to make sure you sat in that seat." Reggie laughed, 'cause they were supposed to be feuding at that time, but they really weren't. It turned out there was nothing wrong with the oxygen supply, and we didn't need the masks after all.

Except for that one incident, the flight was spectacular. We flew over Washington and Oregon and California, and it was a bright night and you could see the snow-capped mountains. I told Thurman how much fun I had had, and he told me that when he got back to New York he would be going over to Teterboro Airport to practice and that I could fly with him and bring my son. A week later in Canton he crashed the plane.

Thurman took his flying very seriously. After ballgames we would often sit around and have a few beers, but if he knew he was going to be flying, he would only have Coke or Pepsi. He wouldn't even have one beer. Unfortunately, Thurman had not been flying all that long, and he moved up to a jet before he was ready. It was too much, too fast.

The night he crashed, there was a knock at my door. It was Catfish Hunter, who lived across the street from me. He said, "Thurman's dead." I said, "What are you talking about?" He said, "Thurman crashed the plane today." It took a few minutes to sink in. I just couldn't believe it. It was the first real tragedy that I had had in my life, and I didn't accept it well. I broke down and cried like a baby.

The funeral, as you might expect, was very sad. To see all those relatives in Canton, especially Diane and his kids, and his in-laws, really made it rough, and we were all teary-eyed as we sat on the bus leaving the graveyard where Thurman had been buried.

Thurman had loved junk food. He could eat a pizza at every meal. Or cheeseburgers. He loved cheeseburgers. As we pulled around the corner from the cemetery, there was a string of junk food joints. I said, "Only Thurman would get buried next to a Burger King and a pizza parlor." We grinned. It was a perfect place for Thurman to be buried.

We can joke about Thurman now, but for a long time we didn't even bring up his name. Now, when we see a fat guy on the street, someone will say, "Hey, look at Thurman." The jokes are a way to ease the pain. And for a while it was tough to concentrate on playing. When his plane crashed, so did our season. We didn't feel much like playing the rest of the year.

When Billy came back, so did the feuding, only this time it was Billy who was on Reggie's side, with George coming down on his star hitter. Then when George saw that Billy and Reggie were getting along real well, he called Billy on the phone to say that Reggie had told him he didn't want to play for Billy. It almost looked like George was trying to get the feud going again.

Toward the end of the year George ordered Billy to say negative things in the papers about Reggie, I suppose because Reggie's contract was coming to an end. Maybe he wanted to downgrade him for the rest of his time as a Yankee so he wouldn't be attractive to other teams. Or maybe George felt Reggie had gotten too big for his britches. Who knows? Whatever the reason, Billy refused.

At the end of the year Al Rosen quit as general manager. George never listened to him much anyway. Rosen was just someone to blame when something George did went wrong.

Billy was also gone—again—before 1979 was out. During the off season he punched out the now-famous marshmallow salesman in Minneapolis, and George fired him, and in 1980 we started the season with Gene Michael as general manager and Dick Howser as manager. Howser did a superb job. We won 103 games, and unfortunately I had to miss the last two months of the season with hepatitis.

I got sick July 23. My blood tests were bad, so they sent me home. Because of the possibility of infection, I couldn't even be around the other players. But they told me to try to come back and get in shape for the playoffs. All summer I had been sitting on the beach in San Diego, and I was rooting hard for us, but I figured that come the playoffs I would be watching on television from my home. Aurelio Rodriguez was doing an excellent job, and I figured they'd stay with Chi Chi.

Before we got Rodriguez, Eric Soderholm had been playing third, and he couldn't handle the pressure at all. I was in the hospital, and Gene Michael called me up and asked me what I thought about our trading for Aurelio Rodriguez. I said, "If you can do it, get him," and they got him, and Rodriguez was as big a reason as any for us winning the pennant that year.

Toward the end of September I got a call from the Yankees: "Do you think you can be ready for the playoffs?" I said I didn't think so. I said, "I still have hepatitis. My tests aren't very good." They said, "We'd like you to come back here and try." So I returned to New York and played the last game of the season. I didn't want to play with the pennant on the line, so I sat out until we clinched it, which was on the last day in the first game of a doubleheader. I asked if I could play the second game, and the first time up I got a hit, and I guess I looked okay, because Howser told me I was starting in the playoffs.

The first time up in the playoffs I hit an inside-the-park home run, and I thought I was going to die, because I hadn't done any running for two and a half months, and quite honestly, I wasn't sure I could even run that far.

We didn't win in the playoffs. That was the playoffs when George became the star of the team. The cameras were on him more than they were on the players. One time I was batting against Dan Quisenberry, and I hit a wicked shot to third, and Brett turned it into a double play, and the camera caught George swearing like a trooper. Around that time we were getting the feeling that the playoffs were no longer the main story. The main story was George. It was as if the Broadway producer had become bigger than his show, more important than his performers. On TV, in the papers, all you were reading about was George.

In 1980 we had won 103 games, which is the most we won all the time I was a Yankee. And then we made the mistake of losing in the playoffs, and that cost Howser his job.

There was a key play. Willie Randolph was on first, and somebody hit a double, and the left fielder overthrew the cutoff man. Our third-base coach, Mike Ferraro, sent

Randolph home, and George Brett, who was in short left field, behind the cutoff man, turned and threw Randolph out at home. It wasn't a bad play on Ferraro's part. He saw the ball going over the cutoff man's head, and he sent the runner home. But all George could see was Ferraro sending him home and Willie getting thrown out. After the game George went up to Ferraro's wife and chewed him out to her. He said, "Your husband fucked up the game for us." And right there George wanted to fire Ferraro and replace him with Don Zimmer.

Howser, to his credit, told George there was no way he was going to fire Ferraro. He told George, "You fire him, and you fire me too." It became a power struggle, and to no one's surprise, George won. Again. When you own the team, you don't lose those too often.

George made the announcement that Howser had quit to take on an unnamed real estate venture in Florida. That was a lie. It was a way to make it look like George hadn't really fired him. Howser became the coach at Florida State University. Of course, George continued to pay him his salary.

I like Howser a lot. He showed enough confidence in me to say, "Even though you missed two and a half months, you're my third baseman in the playoffs." And as he did with everyone else who knows his stuff, George got rid of him. Gene Michael became manager in 1981.

That year was the year of the strike. The owners wanted to get rid of free agency, and we weren't about to give it up. None of us felt the strike was going to last as long as it did. We didn't even think it would go to a strike. It got delayed one time during the year. We were in Toronto, and we had planned on a strike, and Reggie called us and told us there would be an announcement in the morning. We went and played another few weeks, and they still couldn't get anything settled, and we finally went out. We were stuck in Chicago when we went on strike. They threw us out in the street. After the game in South Chicago, they tossed us out of the park. Here we were with our bags and suitcases. We had checked out of our hotel. They said, "Make your own reservations. Do what you want. You have nothing to do with the Yankees as of now." Guys had to hitch rides downtown to Chicago. It's not a real fun thing to do at midnight. We got some rooms and were able to fly home the next day. Most of us stayed around the area for a week, ten days, figuring the strike would be over soon. After ten days I could see it would be a long one, so I went home to San Diego. We knew the owners had bought strike insurance for fifty days, and it's amazing how they settled the strike on the day after their insurance ran out.

Some teams like Minnesota were making money during the strike. Each team was getting something like a hundred thousand dollars a day from the insurance. But the players didn't benefit and when we settled we didn't gain much.

What was important was that the players stuck together. I'm sure not all the players were for the strike. Reggie was our player rep, but he wasn't losing money like the rest of us were. Reggie had gotten paid. He was paid twice a year, January 1 and June 1, so he had already gotten his pay for the year. It seemed strange to the rest of us that our spokesman didn't have anything to lose whether we held out all year or not. Where Reggie had nothing to lose, I had nothing to gain by a strike. It was mostly to benefit the younger players who would be eligible for free agency. And here I am, sitting out, and losing a hundred thousand dollars. You have to admire Marvin Miller, who can take a whole group of players and sell them on the idea of a strike, when it doesn't benefit a lot of us, especially the big-name players. But he got everyone to stick together, and from that point it was worthwhile. It wasn't like what happened with the football players. They all went in different directions when they had their strike. They have a weak union, whereas we have a strong one. And it's all because of Marvin Miller. I know the owners were glad to see Marvin retire, because no matter who takes his place, they figure he's going to be easier to deal with than Marvin.

As a result of the rules adopted because of the strike, we were guaranteed a spot in the playoffs. Whoever was in first place at the time of the strike was in the playoffs. The second half we played five hundred ball. We played a month and a half getting ready for the playoffs. We knew we were in the playoffs, so there was no reason to bust. Psychologically, it was a letdown.

We had a mini-playoff within our division. We played Milwaukee, won the first two games, and then when we lost the next two, George came into the clubhouse and read us the riot act. He really chewed us out, saying that he was going to back up the truck and clear the lot of us away. That's when the fun stopped for me, and for Goose, and perhaps for a couple of the others. Here was this big shipbuilder about to lose in the playoffs to a used-car salesman. He couldn't abide that. So right before the final game, he gave us a chewing out. We won that game, and to this day he thinks he rallied us.

Once we got past Milwaukee, we played Oakland. Oakland had gotten off to a fast start, so they were in first place at the time of the strike, and Kansas City won the second half, so Oakland and Kansas City played each other, and Oakland won. We beat Milwaukee, and then we went out and swept Oakland in three games.

I did poorly against Milwaukee offensively, one for eighteen, but against Oakland I had nine RBIs in three games. I was MVP. And then we got into the World Series, and in the one game I played I played well. I made a diving catch on a ball Garvey hit off Gossage. And then in the second game I broke my thumb diving for a ball. I wasn't able to play the three games in LA that we lost. I played six innings of the final game in New York, but I shouldn't have played at all. My thumb was too sore. I got a couple hits, but the thumb was throbbing.

And who should get all the headlines during that Series? George. He said he got in a fight in an elevator with a couple Dodger fans. The next morning we came down to leave LA to fly to New York, and there were a lot of cameras in the lobby. I was thinking, "There's a lot of equipment here just to film us leaving LA." Then somebody said, "Did you hear about George?" I said, "What happened?" He said, "He got into a fight last night in the elevator." We got on our bus, and we saw all these cameras coming out of the hotel, and there was George walking along as they were filming him. His lip was all puffed up, and his hand was in a cast. It was hilarious to see. My wife and I were sitting on the next-to-last seat on the bus. George always sits in the front.

When he got on the bus, everyone, including me, was laughing and giggling. I was down in my seat so that he wouldn't see me, and finally I got back up, and George was sitting a seat in front of me. He looked at me and said, "Where were you when I needed you?" I said, "George, I was in bed. You told us all to get our sleep."

We came back to New York, where we lost the final game, and he apologized to the fans. And then he got mad at Reggie, because Reggie said, "We don't need to apologize. We don't have anything to be ashamed of. We lost in the World Series. We have nothing to be ashamed of. We have nothing to apologize to the city of New York about."

George got upset. He looked at it like Reggie was starting a mutiny. It gave him another reason to get rid of Reggie.

All that year George was really giving it to Reggie, saying he was washed up, "wasn't the kind of guy he would want a lasting relationship with." And this was the guy, remember, George was dragging around to the 21 Club, inviting to his birthday parties, his closest buddy. George had decided Reggie was no longer valuable property, and George did everything he could to drag him through the mud. Not that Reggie couldn't stick up for himself. But Reggie's a sensitive guy, and this was his first time having the owner come down on him like that.

George was saying these things to get his price down, so maybe Reggie wouldn't ask for so much money. I was rooting for Reggie to get top dollar, whether with the

Yankees or with someone else. Reggie had earned it. My only reservation was that if he stayed it should be as DH. We had better guys in the outfield than Reggie. If he was going to be adamant about playing in the field, I was just as happy to see him go.

Reggie went. So did Tommy John. They tried to turn him into a power pitcher rather than a player who won with finesse. Here's a guy who's been getting by on what he's been doing for fifteen years, and they want to change him. After a couple of bad outings, they told him he was going to be a bullpen pitcher, and he didn't like it, and I don't blame him, and he sounded off about it, said he wanted to get out, and they traded him to California. And on top of that, George told him he was ungrateful for all he had done for his son. I know his four-year-old son got hurt a few years ago, and I don't know exactly what the Yankees did do for him, but it wasn't right for George to throw that back in his face. They weren't talking family affairs, they were talking business. And Tommy is as good a pitcher as he's ever been. He should still be pitching for the Yankees. It was stupid, all the way around.

Gene Michael also went. I enjoyed playing for Gene. I got along great with him. I had been a friend. For some reason he thought he was going to be able to handle George, because he thought he was George's friend. It didn't work out.

George was calling him constantly, trying to get certain people in the lineup. After a while, Gene finally told George, "Fire me or leave me alone." So he fired him, and then he left him alone.

And yet George kept him on the payroll, and he's still

in the organization. He's a scout and advisor on player personnel. He's one of the famous nine guys who vote on George's baseball committee. They have nine votes, and George has ten.

In 1982 we were supposed to be the Team that George Built. He bragged in the papers that all the trades during the off season had been engineered by him. His was going to be a new approach to Yankee baseball. Throughout our history we have been known as the Bronx Bombers, but for the first time, under the leadership of George Steinbrenner, the Yankees were going in for speed, as though we were playing on Astroturf. George had told everyone he couldn't afford to pay Reggie the million a year he wanted, and then he gave a million a year each to his so-called speed men, Ken Griffey and Dave Collins.

George smugly announced that we were going to win the pennant by stealing bases. During spring training he made us wear sweatsuits and run around a lot, instead of play baseball. I told one reporter, "You can now call us the South Bronx Striders." He didn't like that at all.

When we got to spring training, it was pretty clear we didn't have the kind of speed George was bragging about. Also, if you're going to run, you have to have an aggressive manager, and Bob Lemon is not that type, and neither is Gene Michael. When the season started, we hardly ever stole a base.

During spring training, he told the reporters, "This is the best team I ever put together." A week later he traded seven or eight players, shipped them out wholesale. None of the veterans could figure out why. He got rid of Bucky Dent, who was the heart of our infield, and he traded away Ron Davis, who was one of the best middle relief men we ever had. And who did he get for Davis? Roy Smalley, who's a better hitter than Bucky, but not half the fielder. Lou Piniella, Bobby Murcer, Goose Gossage, and I would sit around and try to figure it out.

To make morale even worse, he made us come to spring training two weeks early. He wrote each of us a letter that in essence said, "You're invited, but you better show up." I have a feeling that is one of the reasons he made me captain. He figured I wouldn't show, so he figured if he made me captain, I would have to come. Spring training is too long as it is. All the early practice did was enhance the opportunity for somebody to get hurt. And make all the players resentful. And tire them out at the end of the season.

Not much made sense in 1982. As I said, George paid Dave Collins about a million dollars a year to come here. Collins was a nice kid. His entire career he had been an outfielder, and when he came to New York, George made him a first baseman. Dave is five foot nine. Early in spring training, he said to me, "Don't you think I'm a little short to be playing first base?" I said, "Maybe we can put a couple of phone books under the bag and get you up to where we can see you."

George told everyone that our manager, Bob Lemon, would be there all year, promised Lem he would have the job all year, and two weeks into the season, he was fired. Gene Michael was made manager, and he lasted until August, and he was fired. Clyde King became manager. George never seemed satisfied with who we had. He never let anything stay the way it was. In the middle of the season he decided to dump his concept of the Yankees as a speed team, and he turned over the roster one more time. We must have gone through forty-five different players, and it is impossible to win that way. I once saw a statistic on the 1927 Yankees, the greatest team of them all. They had the same twenty-five guys all year. They went to spring training, management decided who they wanted to keep, and that was it. George is always preaching tradition. Hell, let's get back to tradition and keep the same players together.

George may pride himself on being a hotshot shipbuilder, but when the Yankee ship began going down, George just ran for the lifeboats. He couldn't accept that things had not worked out the way he wanted them to. He couldn't accept the notion that he wasn't the baseball genius he thought he was. His reaction was to blast all his players in the papers.

He ruined Davey Collins. Davey was unsure of himself to begin with, and then he was given a new position, and then he began reading the derogatory things George was saying about him, and by the end of the season he was walking around totally lost.

George was even on Dave Winfield's ass. Dave plays hard every day, and you have to admire him. Winfield, who has a ten-year contract, didn't even blink. When it was clear that the season was a disaster, George decided to pin the blame on Winfield. He took him on, questioned his integrity, questioned a lot of other things about him, but he didn't fold. He came back and had a good year, and he's doing it again this year. Billy ought to rest him every once in a while, because he plays the game so hard. He's out there every day, and he produces.

Last year the fans finally got wise to what George is all about. The "bottom line" finally caught up to him. We were in New York, playing a game against the Angels. Reggie came to bat. Say what you want about Reggie, he is a very exciting ballplayer. Reggie had struck out the first couple times, and George was sitting in the stands behind the dugout gloating.

Then Reggie hit a long home run, reminding the fans what the Yankees were lacking—Reggie's power—reminding them that it was George's decision to let Reggie go. As Reggie was circling the bases, the fans turned on George. They started chanting, "Steinbrenner sucks. Steinbrenner sucks."

After the game he told reporters, "I couldn't believe the New York fans could use such language." It made me laugh. I thought to myself, "Where has he been for all these years? Doesn't he come to the park?" He must live in a dreamworld.

George, after all, was the one who had trained those fans. Over and over he told them, "The only thing that counts is the bottom line." The team was playing poorly, and the fans were picking up on the bottom line.

George had gotten rid of the powerful personalities on the team. But when he did that, he was taking a big chance. In the past he always allowed himself a buffer, someone to take the heat or the blame if things didn't work out. He had Al Rosen, and then Cedric Tallis. But then he let everyone know he was the one calling the shots, making the deals. He figured that when the Yankees won, he would get all the credit. Unfortunately, it didn't quite work out that way, and the fans knew where to point the finger of blame. The result was "Steinbrenner sucks." He underestimated them. He always does. He doesn't give them enough credit for being knowledgeable. They understood exactly where it was at.

13

SEPTEMBER 1983

I must congratulate management for taking a step that just might bring us the pennant. George traded with the San Diego Padres for pitcher John Montefusco, a right-hander who has really shown us something. Montefusco has pitched well for us every time he's played. The only problem is that around the fifth inning he gets a blister on his thumb, and then he has to come out. But for those five innings, he keeps us in the game.

Montefusco once got into a fight with Dave Bristol, the manager, when he was pitching with the Giants. He has the reputation of being something of a flake, but he seems to have fit in very well with our ballclub.

I was very impressed during his first start at Anaheim. He seems to have a real good fastball. He moved the ball around real good, and he beat them. His next start was in Seattle, and he didn't have a good fastball, but he moved the ball around, changed speeds, and kept us in the game. He looks to be a very good pitcher.

There seem to be more junk pitchers in the league than there used to be. We got beat in Milwaukee by a guy named Tom Candiotti. I wonder if he's related to Chris Condiroli from Oakland. As I said before, "Who are these guys?" Candiotti is a pitcher every minor league pitcher should watch and learn from, because they'd see hope for themselves. Here's a guy whose fastball is in the low eighties. He has a slow curve and he throws strikes and doesn't walk anybody. I was telling Dave Garcia, their third-base coach, after the fifth inning, "It's amazing a guy like that can even make it to the big leagues. Normally he wouldn't even get a shot. Not even a look." A scout normally would write as an evaluation, "Below-average fastball. Keep him in the low minors." I don't know how Candiotti ever got the shot, but now he'll stay because he has such good control and moves the ball around well. He got us out pretty easily. We only got four or five hits. He throws like this rookie from Baltimore, Mike Boddicker. Same type of pitcher. A lot of off-speed stuff. All strikes. You don't find that many young guys who are such good pitchers. There are plenty of young, hard throwers, but not good pitchers. Candiotti and Boddicker are certainly two of the better ones. Nine out of ten pitchers are power pitchers. Every time we come up against one of those slop pitchers, like Larry Gura, Geoff Zahn, Tommy John, our timing is way off. And they come at us with such a good motion, it makes their slop that much better. I'd rather face Nolan Ryan every day than face those guys.

Billy had been complaining that he wanted Bobby Meacham called up from Columbus to play shortstop, and they finally called him up, and Billy put him in the game, and with a runner on base, he booted the first ball hit to him. We didn't get the double play, and they got some base hits, and it cost Righetti another heartbreaker.

After the game, George got on the phone and called the Columbus front office. He said, "Don't send us any more players. I've seen enough of them." Roger Erickson, who was pitching at Columbus, told me, "I didn't think they were going to bring any of us up after that phone call."

After losing two in a row to the Brewers, Billy decided that Dave Winfield needed a rest. Dave has been in a horrible slump. In three weeks, he's had four RBIs, three on ground-outs. So Billy gave him a day off, which he ought to do more of because playing 160 games is much too hard on his legs. He's a big man, and he slides hard, and a day off now and then does him good. The newspapers made a big deal about it, which was ridiculous. The papers were saying that if the Yankees had lost the game with Winfield on the bench, Billy was going to be fired. I'm glad we're on the road when they write that garbage. Billy was simply giving him a needed day off.

With Wynegar injured, we've had trouble throwing out runners stealing bases, so Billy started this kid Espino, and he threw out a runner, got a couple of hits, and hit a home run. Billy liked what he saw, and he's keeping him in there ahead of Cerone.

Cerone hurt himself badly with the Yankees. He had one really fine year, and then he sort of went Hollywood. He hit all the discos and got his name in the gossip columns, and he became the Italian Stallion, and he let it all go to his head. The next year he wasn't half the player he was the year before.

It wasn't totally his fault. He wasn't the first, and he won't be the last New York player to get swept up in the New York life. He was hometown boy makes good. His first year I tried to tell him, "Just be careful of where you go and who you're seen with. Don't try to be a regular at any one hangout, 'cause people find out you're there and they'll make a big issue out of it." But he liked to get his name in the gossip columns and see how much publicity he could get. He got a jean ad contract. Maybe he thought everything was going to come easy to him after that. But since then, he's struggled.

There's a trick to playing in New York. I always tried to stay away from the limelight and stay away from the New York scene. I just go to the ballpark and stay out in New Jersey as much as I can. Some guys like the headlines. I don't and I think it's one reason why I've lasted as long as I have. Some guys get swept up in the headlines, and it makes it hard for them to concentrate on what they're here to do: play baseball.

Some guys can grab the headlines and be seen at this place and that place and party all night long and play well. Other guys only think they can. I don't know if Cerone got a big head after the first year, but he hasn't decisions. You can't make everybody happy. Some guys done anything close to that since. He had some injuries. He broke his thumb. He's a good kid and I like him. I wish he were having a better year, but he's got no one to blame but himself.

If Billy stays, I can't see Cerone staying. I said earlier in the year that the two-catcher system wouldn't work. It lasted about three weeks. Rick ended up spending most of the year on the bench.

Goose was pitching against Milwaukee with two outs in the ninth, men on, and the Yankees ahead by a run. Cecil Cooper hit a pop foul down the left-field line that Milbourne went running over for and didn't quite get. Goose's season has been like that. The Goose took a deep breath, and he struck Cooper out no contest to end the ballgame.

After the game Goose said, "In the six years I've been here, nothing has ever been easy as far as I can see. It's always been a struggle."

Recently, Billy has been using Goose and George Frazier out of the bullpen, and no one else. Dale Murray hasn't been used in three weeks. I guess he's in Billy's doghouse because he hasn't pitched very well. It certainly wasn't anything he said. Murray never pops off. I guess Billy just gave up on him. Bob Shirley, Rudy May, Jay Howell, and Matt Keough haven't pitched either. If you're trying to win a pennant, you have to go with your strongest guys.

None of them are very happy about the situation, but that's what the manager gets paid to do, to make those are gonna end up in the doghouse, and they're going to have to put up with it. That's the way of life in baseball.

Murray'll be a free agent at the end of the year, and I doubt they'll re-sign him, because Billy's down on him. He's down on Keough now too. His fastball is gone, and he hasn't had good control.

Shirley has pitched well, but he became a scapegoat when all the other left-handers were doing a better job than he was. He can pitch. He just got into Billy's doghouse and couldn't get out.

Steve Kemp hasn't been playing much, which is a strange deal. I guess Mattingly beat him out of his job.

Kemp was quoted in the press, saying, "Billy and I don't communicate." Once that came out, Billy benched him. It was like Billy was saying, "If we're not going to communicate, you're not going to play." They gave Kemp an awful lot of money not to play. Over a million a year. I don't know why Billy didn't use him more, because Kemp gives a hundred percent all the time.

After he didn't start for about a week, I asked Kemp, "Did Billy say why he's sitting you down?" Steve said, "He didn't say anything to me."

In the old days, when you got benched, you were fighting from year to year for your job, and so guys would really get upset. Now players have long-term contracts, and it's a little bit easier to accept. Not that players are happy about it, but you know you have four years left on your contract. Kemp has a five-year contract worth five million dollars. That can soothe a lot of hard feelings.

Dave Collins was a player who survived because of his

contract. Davey was in awe of everything that was going on in New York. All the publicity, all the excitement. He was over his head. But he had a lucrative, long-term contract, and now he's playing great in Toronto.

Unlike Dave, Kemp has no problems playing in New York. He'll be fine. All he needs is to play.

A large part of Steve's problem is incredible bad luck. He was injured very early in the season when he played with cotton in his ears. Afterward he went into a terrible slump, which probably had something to do with the injury. And then in Milwaukee, he was standing in the outfield during batting practice, and he was hit in the face by a line drive.

The day Kemp got hurt, I wasn't playing, so I didn't go out onto the field for batting practice. All of a sudden the phone rang in the clubhouse. Gene Monahan, our trainer, was told, "Somebody got hurt on the field." Usually when that happens it's a fan who had a heart attack or got hit by a ball. After a couple minutes, word came back up that it was Kemp. They brought him up to the clubhouse. He was laid out on a stretcher, his eye was completely swollen shut. The swelling was getting worse by the minute. He had a big cut under his eye, and his teeth were chipped.

Gene stood with him waiting for the ambulance, which got there within five minutes and took him to the hospital. Then they found out he had a torn retina, and they did laser beam surgery to correct it. I hope he'll be all right. The next day he was able to read an eye chart with 20–80 vision, which is not good, but his eye is all swollen from the blood in it. At least he could see out of that eye.

It's a little scary, because conceivably his career could have been ended right then and there. I'm glad the players are able to get those long-term contracts. It used to be that they would only offer you a one-year contract, and if you were injured, it became your problem when you had to find something else to do. Now the owners are assuming some of the risk, as they should.

Look at all the people George is still paying, names from the past like Gene Michael, Dick Howser, Bob Lemon, Bobby Murcer, who's sitting up in the announcers' booth, Gullett, Catfish, Holtzman. Mayberry is getting his half million: a whole team of guys spread out through the country who he's paying who aren't even playing. It must be a nice write-off for him.

New York is such a big market. There's big attendance, a big television contract, millions in cable revenue, and just the Yankee logo sells enough to pay a lot of guys' salaries. George is doing okay. Don't feel sorry for George.

When we came home from the road we were only five games back. We had a four-game series against the Orioles, and if we were going to make a run for the pennant, this was the time.

Before the first game George ran into Guidry and me in the clubhouse. "It seems every time we have a big game, you're pitching," George said to Guidry. Ron, who doesn't care much for George, said, "You can get someone else if you want." George kind of ignored that and said, "You know that Guidry's gonna hold 'em and we're gonna score some runs and beat them." I said, "See, that man knows his baseball." And it happened just the way he said. He held them, and we scored some runs.

The reporters had all expected me to comment on George's remark. When all I said was, "The man knows his baseball," they didn't quite know how to take it.

The first game of the Oriole series was our most important game of the year. And when we won it, we felt it was going to give us the momentum to sweep the whole series. Guidry started against Scott McGregor, who is another one of those stars George let get away in the infamous Holtzman trade. It's eight years later, and McGregor, Tippy Martinez, and Rick Dempsey may be leading the Orioles to another pennant. George never talks about his bum deals, but that was one of them. Whenever we go out onto the field to face Scotty, we think about where we'd be if we'd had him.

Ken Griffey got up in the first inning and homered. Griffey is a pro who goes out every day and does his job. He has had to learn a new position, but he's been a better first baseman than I thought he would be. Sometimes he's lost out on the field as far as where to play. Sometimes he'll play back, when he should be in for the bunt, and I'll move him. He's dug some balls out of the dirt even the best first basemen would have trouble with. He's done well, for not knowing the position. A lot better than expected.

Ken doesn't say much. He's not one of those guys who

brags about the Big Red Machine like some players who brag about their old teams. The only time he ever gets loud is when he has a beer. Then he'll get real tipsy and incoherent. It doesn't last long, though. Two beers, and he's asleep. Usually when you give him one beer you like to give him two to put him away. He's the cheapest drunk I've ever seen.

I was surprised when he hit that home run against the Orioles, because you don't think of him as a home-run hitter. He played at Cincinnati, which has a small park, and I don't think he ever hit ten home runs in a season. But he's got ten this year, and a few of them have been long ones. He hits left-handers very well. Last year he was hurt and didn't get to play a lot. This year he's hitting a consistent .330. He's an ideal number-two hitter. He doesn't hit into double plays, he pulls the ball. Billy had him hitting fourth and fifth for a while, but he doesn't really belong there because he doesn't drive in enough runs. He only has about forty RBIs.

We were tied three to three in the eighth against the Orioles. There were 47,000 people in the stands. I knew the series was going to be an important one. I knew we were going to have big crowds, and I knew there'd be a lot of press. I knew that everyone was aware that my contract was up. I knew it would be a good time to have a good series. And I hit two doubles, and in the ninth I hit a home run that won it.

Scotty threw me a ball that might have been over my head, and boom, I swung and hit it into the right-field stands. I was ecstatic. Because it won the game for us, because it showed people I can still play this game.

After the game, everyone was up. We thought we had a good chance of sweeping. I could see the momentum going all the way. We were ready.

The next day we played a doubleheader. In the first game the score was two to two going into the ninth. Shane Rawley started and was pitching beautifully, but Smalley started the ninth by throwing a grounder over Griffey's head for an error, and when Todd Cruz sacrificed the runner to second, Billy brought in Goose. Goose had gotten saves the last five games he pitched, and we were all expecting him to do it again, but after he went oh and two on Dempsey, he walked him, and then he gave up a single to Joe Nolan for a run. The next batter popped up, but Cal Ripken, who has had an all-world year, followed with a double that hit within six inches of the right-field line. I remember earlier in the year Baltimore beat us when they brought in some catcher from the minor leagues who hit a bloop down the left field line to beat us. And here's Ripken doubling six inches fair in the right-field corner. Billy had Goose walk Eddie Murray intentionally to load the bases, and then John Lowenstein hit the ball out about 450 feet.

Shane should have come away with a two to nothing win. He was the bad-luck pitcher. There were six unearned runs because of Roy's error.

Goose felt horrible. Usually, if it's just one run, he'll come in and throw his glove around. After that inning, he just came in and quietly sat down.

After that ninth inning in the first game, things just seemed to steamroll against us. In the second game we were flat, and against Boddicker, we looked bad. I doubled in a run in the first inning, and that was the only run we got. Omar Moreno dropped an easy fly ball and that cost us.

Then on Sunday, Righetti pitched his only bad game of the year. His arm was bothering him, and he was knocked out in the second inning. Todd Cruz, who was hitting .197, beat him with a hit. Rags threw him a changeup, which was a good pitch to throw in that situation, but he got it up and right over the plate, and Cruz hit it. It makes you feel bad when a guy like Cruz beats you. With all the good hitters they have, here's a guy hitting .190, and you figure he's an easy out, and he ends up beating us.

But the Orioles are good. They're a good ballclub. They platoon a lot, and each guy knows and accepts his role. They know when they're going to be in the lineup and when they won't be. Unlike us.

After we won the first game of the Baltimore series, all the reporters were talking about how this was like '78 and how the Yankees were going to come back, but in truth, the reporters didn't know what they were talking about. There's a big difference between '78 and now. In '78 Boston was fading as we were coming on. This year we're playing a team as hot as, or hotter than, we are.

Our team is disorganized, and right now the front office is blaming Billy. But the way I see it is the problem stems from the fact that the front office signed so many players before they signed Billy. They said, "Here, Billy, you figure out a way to put all these players on the field.'' They ought to let the manager help make up the personnel on the club. George makes up his mind who he wants without consulting the manager. The smartest way to conduct business would be to first sign your manager and then with his help go about signing up your players. They should have hired Billy and then said, ''Billy, who are the players you would like to get?'' It doesn't work well any other way.

Had Billy not been the manager this year, had Gene Michael, say, been the manager, I would have been wherever George Steinbrenner told him to play me. In fact when I saw Gene Michael a week ago, he said, ''You surprised me. I didn't think you could have the year you're having.'' I said, ''A lot of people didn't think so. But Billy thought I could, and I did.'' A lot of people had given up on me, Gene Michael being one of them. If he had been manager again, I'm sure that Smalley would have been playing third, and I would have been sitting on the bench. It wouldn't have set too well with me. I don't know what I would have done.

By the end of the Baltimore series, we were resigned to second place. Which is not to say that we are giving up. We still have to go out there and win in order to finish second. And if we do win and something happens to Baltimore, we've got a shot. The trouble is, if Baltimore loses now, they're going to be losing to Detroit and to Milwaukee, while we're beating Cleveland and Boston, so it's almost impossible for us to finish first. The mood of the team is, ''It's over.'' But we also feel that we gave it a hell of a shot.

After Baltimore we played a series against the Brewers, and before the first game George came in and gave us a speech. He said, "I know it's going to be tough for us to win. It's not impossible. It can happen. But whatever you do, go out and try to get second place. If we get second place and show we're better than Detroit and Milwaukee, we can still hold our heads high and feel like winners."

It was a very professional attitude on George's part. You never know what to expect from the man. Before he came in, we didn't know whether he was going to chew us out for losing or give us one of those "You guys are all gone" speeches, which he's done before.

It was a very good talk. George seems to have grown. I think he realizes we can't win every year. And yet I still think he believes that just because he pays his players more than the other teams we should win. I hope someday he will realize that money doesn't always buy the best players, and that putting twenty-five all-stars on a team will not always bring you a pennant.

After the Baltimore series Phil Pepe of the *Daily News* already had Billy fired. He wrote. "Too many players quit on the manager this year." I don't know where he gets that from. I don't know who he was referring to. That's the trouble when they write things like that. If a writer alleges that "the players have quit on the manager," he should be required to name names or to give specific reasons why a particular player feels the way he does. I haven't seen anybody quit on him, not at all. You'd be a fool to quit. You're sitting there staring at a manager who has a four-year contract. Why would you quit on a manager like that? All it does is affect what he's going to do the next year. What may be true is that Billy feels that there are a number of players who aren't winners, and as a result those players have ill feelings toward Billy.

And this goes back to an earlier question, "How is Billy expected to win when you keep trading for guys coming from losing organizations?"

It takes time to become a winner.

I went from a winning organization in Minnesota to a losing organization in Cleveland and then to New York. I was coming from a loser, and it took me a while to get accustomed to what it takes to win. When you play for a losing team too long you take losing for granted. It takes a couple of years of playing through pennant races to learn how to win. In '74 we had a pennant race that went down to the final day. You go through something like that, and it makes it easier to handle the pressure. The Baltimore players went through a pennant race last year, right down to the final day, with Milwaukee. And as far as experience is concerned, that's the same thing as winning it. If you play 162 games and only lose by one, you've been through it, as a winner.

But to do this, you have to maintain the nucleus of a team for at least three years so the players can get used to one another and play together as winners.

That's how the Dodgers do it every year. That's how Baltimore's doing it. That's how Milwaukee does it. Kansas City. St. Louis. But we don't do it that way. The only everyday players left from our winning team in 1978 are myself and Randolph. Piniella isn't a regular anymore. George always likes what he sees in a player from another organization, and he grabs the player without knowing whether he will fit in or not.

To be a player in this organization is very frustrating. I would have loved to see our infield of myself, Bucky, Willie, and Chambliss still here. We would have been an awfully strong ballclub if they had stuck the four of us together for seven or eight years. But it just didn't happen.

Our outfield will be fine if George leaves them together. An outfield of Kemp, Winfield, and Moreno or Mattingly is excellent, if he leaves them there for a while, but who knows if he will.

For the second day in a row the *Daily News* attacked Billy, saying he should be fired and I, of all people, should become the manager. It was funny, because after the game, Billy told reporters, "I asked Nettles on the bench what I should do, and Nettles told me to bring in Goose, so I brought in Goose." Billy was making light of the whole thing.

I got a pretty good ribbing when I came into the clubhouse. Guys were calling me "skip." "How you doing, skip? Can I be in the lineup today, skip?"

I came into the clubhouse and I said to Billy, "It looks like I'm after your job, huh, skip?" He smiled. He said, "Goddamn, I better be on my toes."

It said in the newspaper article that I should have a dugout aide like Zimmer or Yogi. Zimmer came up to me before the game and joked, "Now you forget about the bad game I had when I had those two guys thrown out. Just forget about that, okay?"

I found the article kind of funny because Bill Madden had written that "George has been ominously silent about his manager for next year." Why should George even be talking about it? Billy has a four-year contract. The press is putting pressure on George to force him into making a decision he doesn't even have to make.

Still I was flattered by the article. Maybe publicity like this will make George sit up and take notice as to my importance on the Yankees. Maybe it will push him to sign me again or think twice about letting me go. I don't know. It can't hurt. Other clubs have also begun to show interest in me. Moss Klein wrote an article in the *Newark Star Ledger* saying that the Red Sox want me very badly.

In any case, George has finally agreed to talk a two-year contract. Earlier in the year he said, "We'll talk one year," and within the last week he told my agent he'll talk a two-year extension. He's got to pay me right for me to stay around. I want to be paid in line with the salaries on this club. If I went to another team, like the Red Sox, I'd have to take into consideration their salary structure. Our salary structure is such that George would have to pay me a lot more than most other clubs. A lot of teams are looking for a third baseman. Look at Baltimore. They have a third baseman hitting .198. Look at the White Sox. They are winning their division by twenty games, and they have a third baseman hitting .230. There are clubs out there. Toronto was interested in me last winter. There's no reason they shouldn't be interested this year.

So maybe an article like this might get George to thinking that he should sign me.

Goose told me yesterday, "If you're player-manager, I promise I won't leave you." He was joking. Goose and Billy get along okay, but he seems to think it's not as much fun playing on the Yankees as it would be playing somewhere else. It has to do with the problems he had with George last year. All the petty things from George have pissed him off an awful lot. Also, he hasn't come in and shut the door on teams like he has in the past, and he's frustrated about that. It's his option year, so for him it's even more important that he do well and I'm sure that extra pressure hasn't helped him.

It's funny, because on one hand the *Daily News* is

complaining that Goose has been terrible, and on the other hand they are saying that the Yankees can't do without him. Where would we be without Goose? We still have confidence that he will come in and do the job. I do, and I know that Billy does. I can't see anyone else in our bullpen who you would want to come in and preserve a lead in the eighth or ninth inning.

I think George is trying to get something on Billy so he can fire him. As a result, Lou Piniella got caught up in the middle of an incident he didn't like at all.

Murray Cook and Steinbrenner called Lou up to the office to find out if the players were happy with Billy, and it really upset Lou that they would try to get him to undermine the manager. Lou said, "You're not paying me to evaluate the manager. You're paying me to play and be the batting coach. You have all these so-called executives to make these decisions. Don't get me involved."

Lou went and told Billy about it. Billy told me, "They tried to get Lou to go up to the office to tell them bad things about me." Billy said, "I went up and reamed Murray out, called him a few names and told him, 'Don't try to undermine my ballclub again.' "

Back in '77 and '78, players were running up to Gabe Paul and to Steinbrenner all the time. I wasn't one of them. I was never one of their favorites. Billy never had to worry about my being one of their pipelines. They know how I feel about the front office.

Somehow the papers never got hold of this one, and it's good because they could really blow it up and put Lou and Billy on the spot. That's what sells newspapers, George versus Billy. They would love to get them at each other's throats again, two volatile people. Just give George the excuse to fire Billy, or give Billy the excuse to quit. Even though Billy has a four-year contract, it would not surprise me if Billy got fired. As everyone knows, George has bitten the bullet on a few contracts.

I have never figured out why it is so difficult for George and the manager to work together. I wish I knew. They always seem to be at odds with each other. Unless George gets a yes-man. The manager has to use the players. It's only logical that he should have the loudest voice in determining who those players are. But that's not the way it is on the Yankees. The front office signs a bunch of players and says, "Here they are. You win with them or else." That's why it would seem ideal that the manager also be the general manager. Whitey Herzog was doing that with St. Louis. Billy had that at Oakland, yet he still got in trouble with the owners. Billy is going to have trouble wherever he goes. He doesn't like authority over him. Even if he were an owner, he'd find some way to get himself in trouble.

I was watching a documentary on Douglas MacArthur the other day. The whole time I was watching it, all I could think of was Billy. MacArthur was a guy who became famous for orders he went against. If somebody told him to do something, he did the opposite, because he felt he was right and knew best. The whole time I was watching that I was thinking, "Here's the guy Billy must have patterned his life after." Billy will always be remembered for doing things he wasn't supposed to do. Fighting with Reggie or George or the Marshmallow Salesman. MacArthur said, "I will return," and he returned. Billy always returns too, it seems.

Out of the blue, the three New York newspapers quoted "a reliable source close to the Yankees" as saying that the "Yankee players are on the verge of rebellion because of Billy Martin." They reported that players such as Cerone, Griffey, Goose, Kemp, May, and Murray, and coach Don Zimmer, were all unhappy and wanted to leave because of Billy. The "reliable source" was quoted as saying that George is feeling pressure to fire Billy because of player dissatisfaction.

What was funny about those articles was that all three came out the very same day. Here were Bill Madden in the *News,* Murray Chass in the *Times,* and Henry Hecht in the *Post* all knocking Billy and quoting "sources close to the Yankees." If I were a suspicious person, I would almost think that George was up to his old tricks again.

Articles like this would give George a ready-made excuse to get rid of Billy. I don't know a better way to get rid of a manager than to say most of the players are dissatisfied. For him to plant a story like that wouldn't be exactly ethical, but I wouldn't put it past him.

The thing that never fails to amaze me is that whenever "a source close to the Yankees" is quoted, he never is identified, which is the chickenshit way of giving a statement. And worse, the reporters also take the chickenshit way out by allowing "a source close to the Yankees" to get away with it.

This way anyone can say anything he wants, no matter how rotten or nasty, because no one will know for certain who said it. If you're going to say something against somebody, at least have the balls to allow yourself to be quoted. And if a reporter is going to write something nasty, he should have the balls to say who said it. Otherwise, who knows what the truth is?

Also, this way a writer can make up a statement and attribute it to an unnamed source. And I don't put it past a couple of the writers who cover the Yankees to use their own ideas and then write that some "source" said it.

It seemed funny, all three papers coming out suddenly blasting Billy, saying there are players who want to leave the Yankees because of him.

Reading it in the papers was the first I had heard about it. I didn't know all those guys were so unhappy. I knew some of them were unhappy about their playing status. Like Kemp. I know some guys feel Billy doesn't use them enough, like Cerone. I didn't know Griffey was unhappy. I didn't know Rudy was unhappy, although he hadn't pitched much, but that was because of his back. It was a shock to me. I guess those guys waited until we were out of the pennant race to let their feelings be known, but geez, I don't know what they thought they were going to find once they got to the Yankees. They act like they're shocked to see the situation over here. It's really ridiculous. Guys sign big contracts to play in New York, and then they act like they didn't know what was going to happen to them after they get here. Did they think we were going to win 140 games, win the pennant, not have any controversy, and be happy? That hasn't been the history of this club. All they had to do was check it out a little bit and they would have discovered that it's never going to be easy playing here. That's why they are paid such big money. They should have known what they were getting into when they came.

I don't need to go in and reassure Billy that I'm in his corner. I know he's in my corner, too, and he doesn't have to communicate that with me. This is another way the game has changed: these new players think they have to be communicated with. It all started with the movie *Cool Hand Luke*, where the warden says to Paul Newman, "What we have here is a failure to communicate." Everyone picked up on that, and now in the papers you read about players who say to themselves, "If I'm having trouble in baseball, I'll blame it on a lack of communication with the manager." That's a copout. I could get along fine if my manager never spoke to me for months at a time. Put my name in the lineup and play me. You can even rest me once in a while. But I don't need a manager talking to me every day. Some of these other players just use it as an excuse for not playing up to their potential.

Earlier in the year Griffey said it. "We haven't communicated all spring." Now it's Kemp who says he and Billy aren't communicating. What the hell is a manager supposed to do? When I started playing, the manager wouldn't come up and pat you on the back for months at a time. He was the boss. It's the same in every business. How many times a month does your boss tell you you're doing a great job? You get a paycheck. That's thanks enough. In baseball the only communication you need is to look at the lineup and read if your name is on it. That's communication. Some of these guys are making a million dollars a year, and they want to be talked to. It's beyond me.

If I was the manager, this would be my communication: I would say to the guys on the bench, "Stop second-guessing me and stop bitching." Any time a player is on the bench, he's saying to the guy sitting next to him, "Why didn't we hit-and-run? Why didn't we bunt? Did you ever see a stupid move like that?" Here's my communication: "Shut the hell up or get the hell out." Any time you have twenty-five guys, some of them are going to be unhappy, and they're going to backstab the manager. Maybe the answer would be to reduce the roster to eighteen. That way there would be fewer players sitting on the bench bitching.

I have never heard guys openly griping about Billy. All the griping seemed to have been in the press, which makes me wonder even more whether George was the one behind the stories.

The papers mentioned a confrontation between Billy and Griffey over Griffey's kids in the clubhouse. The kids were out in the hallway one day. There are always ten or fifteen kids out there, playing ball, and we had had a tough loss, and Billy heard all the noise, and he told the clubhouse man, "Would you go down and tell all those kids to keep it a little quiet." The man went over to Griffey's locker and said, "Hey Griff, will you tell your kids to keep it down." Griffey thought Billy had said something about his kids, and he really didn't. It was just a misunderstanding.

My feeling is that Griff was annoyed it took the Yankees so long to give him his regular job at first base, that all his career he's been an outfielder, and what was he doing playing first when he's an outfielder? Which is a good question, but it falls in line with all the other free agents George signs and switches. He'll give a guy like Winfield a million dollars a year and move him from right field to left. He did it to Collins. He moved him from the outfield to first base. He moved Kemp from left field to right field. He moved Smalley from short to first base. Every time he signs a free agent, he tries to change his position. If I was an owner and gave a guy a million dollars a year, he would have to be the best at his position, and I would leave him at that position. It's kind of bizarre, actually. But this isn't Billy's doing. Why do the reporters always take the owner's side? Take what they're writing about Goose, for instance, that Goose won't come back because of Billy. I don't see anyone writing that Goose won't come back because George has taken an awful lot of the fun out of the sport.

I'm sure George is a Vince Lombardi fan from way back. "Winning is everything," but that's a bunch of bullshit. There are different ways of going about winning, and in my opinion there is only one way to win: by having fun. The only reason anybody plays baseball in the first place is that it is fun. So why should you get all serious about it just because you're getting paid to play?

You can look across to the Oriole dugout and see the fun those guys are having. They laugh around the batting cage, you can see them laughing at things in the dugout during the game. Everything around us is so tense all the time. You always have an idea that somebody—George or one of his people—is watching you, and that if he sees you laughing or cutting up, then he'll come down hard on you. And this is a large part of the reason a guy like Goose wants to go somewhere else.

Not that Goose is totally happy with Billy either. A couple of years ago Goose got on Art Fowler, and Art went and told Billy, and Billy, who had had a few drinks, came up to Goose's room and challenged him to a fight. Goose said, "No, I'm not going to fight you. I don't have anything to gain by fighting you, Billy." The next day Billy didn't mention it. I don't know whether he remembered it or not. He was probably embarrassed that it had even happened, but the incident was unfortunate. Goose also doesn't like the fact that Billy took over as pitching coach when Art Fowler got fired, instead of letting Sammy Ellis or Torborg, or someone who knows pitching, run things. Those guys sit out in the bullpen for nine innings, and I'm sure they do a lot of bitching and griping, 'cause any time you get seven or eight guys together in the pen, there's going to be at least three guys not happy with their status.

I know that Goose isn't happy with the turmoil that goes on. The writers say he feels he isn't warmed up enough when he comes into a game, but he never said that to me.

I think Goose is going through a bad year, and he has to let his emotions out against somebody. If he were paid a top salary, I think he would stay put. If I stay I will do my darndest to see that he does. The problem is that I don't know if I'm going to stay. Right now, they've let the thing go so long that Goose would be a fool not to test the free agent market.

If I'm not signed by the end of the year, I'll declare my free agency. I'd like to sit down and settle it with George, but with only two weeks left in the season, it doesn't look like we will.

I think what he's going to do is wait until the last day of the season and try to sign me. Two or three months ago he could have signed me for a lot less. At the beginning of the season, if he had renewed my contract for a year, I would have signed it. But I've had a good year, and now the price has gone way up. And I don't know if he'll want to pay it.

I've been with the Yankees for eleven years. I deserve some consideration. But the only word he understands is leverage. If you have leverage, you get money out of him. As far as loyalty goes, it doesn't mean anything.

Last year the Yankees finished three games under five hundred, and this year we're seventeen games above five hundred, and all the writers are saying how bad we were this year and that Billy should be fired. I don't understand it. Billy should be given a medal. The team was so screwed-up last year that it would have been impossible to turn it around in one year.

This year Baltimore kept winning and winning and winning. They never went into a prolonged slump even though they had their share of injuries. They had pitching that was hurting early in the year. Yet they got steady performance out of a few key guys, and Joe Altobelli platooned very well in a couple places, and the players seemed to accept their roles.

People in the Yankee organization are always impatient. The Yankees signed Rick Reuschel, and then after he got hurt, they wouldn't wait for him to heal, and they gave him his release. The Cubs signed him, and he looks like he's going to be a very good pitcher again. George's crack baseball committee is so impatient. If you don't show what you can do today, they don't want to wait until next month.

Doyle Alexander just won his fifth game for the Toronto Blue Jays. When he was with us, he couldn't pitch well at all. And because we had too many guys, we essentially gave Mumphrey away. We pay a fortune for players like these, and instead of taking our time and then making a big blockbuster deal for one player, we give them away.

It's very frustrating for me to go out there knowing the problems that exist on the Yankees. You look at the lineup every day, and it's a surprise just to see who's going to be playing. I can see it on players' faces when they look at the lineup card. They wonder, "Why aren't I in there?" or "Why am I hitting where I'm hitting?" "Why is so-and-so playing and I'm not?" You can see it on their faces. There are too many players who don't know what their role is. They don't belong here. They belong where they can play every day.

Even Baylor has been confused. He's used to playing every single day, batting against everybody. And he's been benched several times against right-handed pitching. A DH doesn't need a rest. How can a DH be tired?

Winfield should also play 150 games a year. And Kemp. He's proved he can play every day. Then we have Mattingly. He should be playing, because he's proved he can hit big league pitching.

As far as the outfield, I would put Kemp in right, Griffey in center, and Winfield in left and DH Baylor, platoon Mattingly and Balboni at first base, put Randolph at second, Andre at short, and me at third. Wynegar is having a better year than Cerone, so I would go with him as catcher. That would be my solution. I would go with that lineup every day. Let the other big stars go and get the pitching that we need. It'll be tough to do. I hope we keep Oscar Gamble. Oscar is a wonderful guy to have on the club. You don't need an awful lot of pinch-hitters in the American League. Still we ought to keep Oscar, and I don't think we will. He won't want to stay here. Piniella might be finished. He has an inner-ear infection that just might end his career.

Our starting pitchers are excellent. We have Guidry, Righetti, and Rawley, and Montefusco and Fontenot have been pitching great for us. They're a little tired now. Most of these guys have never pitched so many innings in a season. I hope Billy gives them some time off. I hope he doesn't listen to George about how important it is to win the rest of the games. He'd be much better off looking at some of the young pitchers.

As for next year, George has to sign Goose, and he has to find someone to set the game up for Goose the way Davis used to. And he has to sign me.

This is Billy's first year with basically new personnel. He's learning that maybe he didn't handle Goose just right. Maybe he'll learn to let him start an inning rather than always bring him in with runners on base. There's really little this team needs besides patience.

It was interesting to see how much better Smalley played after Robertson got hurt. Before, he didn't know whether he'd be in there or not, and he was uncertain in the field. After Andre got hurt and Smalley knew he'd be in there every day, it was like he was a different player. His range wasn't any better, but he wasn't beating us in ballgames like he had been doing before.

Still, nobody's going to beat Baltimore. Baltimore is perfect. Everyone knows his role and is comfortable and happy in that role. They get along with their manager. Their manager isn't domineering like Billy. They've accepted their roles, and they've gone out and beaten the hell out of everybody.

I thought it would take ninety-two wins in our division, because everyone is so good, but they are going to win a hundred games. You got to take your hat off and say, "We got beat by a much better team." Not necessarily by more talent. But by a better team.

14

OCTOBER 1983

Yesterday the season ended, I got my last paycheck, and today I'm unemployed for the first time since I started playing ball eighteen years ago.

I'd be a little worried if I didn't know there were a bunch of teams looking for third basemen, and since I had a productive year, I don't think I have much to worry about. As long as somebody wants me, I'll be ready.

I sit and picture myself in other uniforms. I wonder what it would be like to hit in Fenway Park for a couple years. Or Baltimore. Or Detroit. I see a lot of teams that are looking for third basemen. I just wonder why our guy hasn't made me an offer.

Meanwhile, the papers are still hot with the story that Billy is going to get fired because the players are unhappy. Since we dropped out of the pennant race, it seems everybody's complaining. I hadn't heard it, but I don't suppose they would have gone to the papers if they didn't feel that way.

Of course, George should know by now that if you hire Billy to manage, you can't have guys like Clyde King and Gene Michael from the front office telling him what to do and you can't expect him to listen to coaches who aren't loyal to him. You fire Art, to piss Billy off and get him to quit, and what do you expect him to do? There's no way he's going to listen to front office coaches like Ellis and Torborg. So now the pitchers are pissed off at Billy. But if I were a pitcher, I'd be mad at George for getting rid of Art in the first place. Art was a great buffer between Billy and the players. They could talk to Art if they had problems, and Art could talk to Billy, and Billy would listen to him.

Once again George has set up a situation against Billy like he did in '78 with Reggie. Under the present circumstances, if so many players are as unhappy with Billy as they say, then it would not be wise for him to come back. But if George allowed Billy to choose his own coaches and to have a say in the makeup of the team, Billy would probably take the team to the pennant. Under the system we have now, I don't think anyone can successfully manage the Yankees. George tried it with his yes-men, like Gene Michael, Bob Lemon, and Clyde King, and he tried it with Billy, and it didn't work either way.

Being the Yankee manager is a lot like being the wife of Henry the Eighth—there's a lot of prestige, and the money and the trappings are very nice, but you don't get to keep the position for very long. The one difference is that George's managers live to tell about it.

The Yankees will never be winners again if George doesn't let a knowledgeable baseball man actually run the operation. He lets his emotions run the club, and it's not the way to do it. There are too many other professionally run organizations in our division. I imagine their general managers love to go one-on-one with George in a baseball deal. I just hope he listens to some baseball people before he makes his decisions about next year. The last baseball person he listened to was Gabe Paul. Since then we haven't won, except by a fluke in '81, when we were handed a playoff spot because of the strike.

The way things are going it looks like I'm going to go into the free agent draft. Nine days after the end of the World Series, you have to declare your free agency. Then the draft is November 7. Up until that time the Yankees still have a chance to sign their own players. But they haven't made me an offer yet.

The one thing that makes me think he might sign me is that he hasn't run me down in the papers like he did Reggie when he let him go. He humiliated Reggie, said he was washed-up, was a bad person. Maybe it'll be my turn in the next couple of weeks. I don't know. It would be pretty hard to do. I played the best I played in the last four years. Still at this point I would be surprised if he did make an offer.

I've been a Yankee for eleven years, and I would like very much to remain with the team, despite whatever has gone on between me and George. I think of myself as playing for the New York Yankees, not for George Steinbrenner. There's something special about playing for the Yankees. When I go back home to San Diego, people say, "Hey Graig, I know you. You play for the New York Yankees," and that means a lot to me.

And yet I don't want to feel that I'm being taken ad-

vantage of. Moss Klein in the *Newark Star Ledger* wrote
that I was only twelfth in salary on the Yankees.

George set a salary structure on this club, I didn't, and
to keep me he's going to have to pay me toward the top of
that structure. I've been one of his top players. I'm third
in RBIs and third in home runs, and third is third, so pay
me right behind Winfield and Kemp. He doesn't understand that, though. I play offense and defense, whereas
he pays some guys just to play defense or offense. And
then there are a lot of guys he pays a lot just to sit on the
bench, and that doesn't include the guys he pays to sit at
home.

The Yankee tradition may be important, but that important it's not. In the end, it's the same game, whether
you play in Boston or New York or Baltimore. After all,
the most important thing is playing. There are some guys
who said, "If the Yankees don't want me, I'll just quit."
That's not me. I hope it's the Yankees, but if not, it'll be
somebody else.

What I love about the game of baseball is that
whether you win or lose, it's still so much fun. You go
out on the field, and you're using your body to do
something that you love to do. You learn it when
you're four or five, and you're able to do it until you're
in your forties, and every day is different and exciting
and something to look forward to. There are peaks and
valleys, and even when you're mired in one of the valleys, it's still fun.

It's a game. Not a business. They don't advertise that
there's going to be a business meeting between the Boston Red Sox and the New York Yankees today. They say

there's going to be a game between the Red Sox and the Yankees. That's why it's fun.

George has tried to change that. He would love for the headlines to read: "Big Business Meeting Today Between Boston and New York." That would please him no end. But no matter how much he fights to change it, it will always be a game, the game that I love to play.

15

DECEMBER 1983

I was one minute away from becoming the "former third baseman of the Yankees" when George and my agent, Jerry Kapstein, agreed to a new contract—two years, just like I wanted, at a million a year, just like I wanted. Under the rules, George had until three days before the free agent draft—until midnight of November 4—to sign me, and for a long while there, it didn't look like it was going to happen.

Then just three days before the deadline, George came out to San Diego to talk to Kapstein about me and Goose. He brought Gene Michael with him. Jerry and I went down to the hotel where George was staying, and the four of us met.

Before we went into the meeting, Jerry told me, "Now, George is going to be the nicest person in the world to you. He's going to build you up, praise you, have nothing but great things to say about you." I didn't know what to think about that, because that had never happened before. We walked in, and we were there for about an hour, and it was just like Jerry said. George made it sound like I was the greatest player who ever played the game. It was something I wasn't prepared to hear. I was sure he was again going to tell me I was over the hill, was washed up, and was asking for too much money. What he said was, "You're right. You deserve the money you're asking for. But I just can't pay it to you."

I said, "If I'm going to stay with the Yankees, you're going to have to pay it or else I'll go somewhere else." He said, "You're not going to get that kind of money somewhere else." I said, "I know that." And it kind of took him aback. He said, "What do you mean?" I said, "I know nobody else will pay me the money I'm asking you to pay. I don't expect Baltimore or Boston to pay me the money I'm asking from you. But if I'm going to stay here, I'm going to fit in with your salary structure. If I go to another club, I'll be willing to fit in its salary structure. I want to be close to the top." George said, "I don't understand you athletes. You would take two or three hundred thousand dollars a year less to play somewhere else?" I said, "Yeah. If it has to be that way." He didn't know what to say after that.

Before he left San Diego, he said, "I'll get back to you with an offer in a couple of days." And he did. He called Jerry back and made an offer, and it was only for one year for about seven hundred thousand. I said, "No. It has to be two years for a total of two million." He said, "We can't do it." The next day—the day of the deadline—he finally made the offer, with everything included coming to a little over two million dollars. In one day, he came up with an additional million and a half dollars. I guess he was just trying to wait me out.

I had been talking to other teams. Baltimore said it would draft me. You couldn't talk money with the other teams until after the draft, but you could find out who was interested. Boston was interested. The Padres were interested. We talked to Toronto and Detroit. Kansas City was definitely interested. So was San Diego. I had lunch with Ballard Smith of the Padres the day I signed. I knew he wouldn't pay me what I was asking from George. But George didn't know that. He couldn't be sure. George told me there would be no interest. He said, "We've been asking around, and there are no clubs interested in you." He was trying to scare us into accepting whatever offer he was going to make. We said, "You'd be surprised how much interest there is."

I had thoughts of coming home to San Diego to play. I knew the Padres were looking for a power-hitting third baseman. I would have fit perfectly into their plans for a couple of years.

I got back after the lunch with Ballard, and George had finally made a decent offer, and we decided to accept it right then rather than go on through the draft. Because it was my intention all the time to stay with the Yankees—if I could be paid right. I didn't have the big ego thing of going through the draft to find out exactly what my worth was. I knew what I wanted and where I wanted to play. The offer was there, so I took it.

We signed with telegrams. I looked at my telegram,

and it was marked 11:59. One more second, and I'd have been gone.

I guess George got tired of having to take a back seat to Billy again. I can't think of any other reason why he fired him. Billy had done everything George had asked him to do. He improved our record, and he helped increase attendance by three hundred thousand. But when Billy signed his four-year contract to be manager, one of the things he made George promise was that he would keep away from the players, stop making suggestions, in short, butt out. And George did that for a year. And it must have just killed him to be so quiet. Now George can reconnect the phone to the dugout. Now he can come back into the clubhouse to give more of his rah rah speeches.

Actually, in the end it might end up better for us with Yogi as manager. Billy would be fine if George would only leave him alone, stop putting even more pressure on him than he puts on himself. But George won't stop, so the pressure cooker inside Billy boils up, and by the end of the season Billy is so high-strung that you can hardly talk to him. I'm sure that's why so many of the guys said they were having such a hard time communicating with Billy. During the final month, Billy was ready to explode. It was a miracle George didn't cause him to have a nervous breakdown.

With Yogi as manager, I'm sure playing will be a lot less tense, a lot more fun. Yogi doesn't put pressure on the players the way Billy does. He leaves everyone alone. Yogi will still have to deal with the problem of where to play all the stars we have, but at least he will consult his pitching coaches, Jeff Torborg and Sammy Ellis, so the pitchers will be much happier. The big frustration will be to sit back and watch George try to push Yogi around while he tries to manage the Yankees. Yogi knows his baseball, is well respected, and has a record of winning. But he has never played for George before.

I'm going to miss Goose terribly. Goose was sick of George, and he decided he wanted to go somewhere fun. I couldn't help shaking my head when George told reporters that Goose had left because he didn't want to be held responsible for George's firing Billy. George also said Goose had left because the fans had booed him. George forgot to tell reporters the real reason Goose left: George.

Maybe everything will work out for next season after all. I was happy to see that instead of rushing out to sign three new expensive free agents, George has apparently decided to listen to his general manager, Murray Cook, and concentrate on resigning the players he was in danger of losing to free agency. We didn't have a bad team in 1983. With a year of having played together under our belts, I expect that we will be even stronger in 1984. We could even win the pennant.

All we have to do is fine-tune this team just a little bit. I was sorry to see Balboni go, but at least he'll get a chance to play now. And we got Mike Armstrong, an excellent young arm for our bullpen. With Goose gone, somebody will step in and do the job. Now just let the manager manage, let the general manager handle the trades. And then George should sit back and let us play. Don't second-guess. Don't mess us up. And we'll win.

All we need from George is a fighting chance.

EPILOGUE

When BALLS was published in the spring of 1984, most reviewers complained that the book was but "300 pages of unrelieved criticism." It was as though there was something inherently wrong with a ballplayer airing his dissatisfaction with the way things were being run. None of these critics cited what clearly was the most unusual aspect of this book: Here was a major league ballplayer, in this case the captain of the team, publicly making a statement about what was wrong with his team's management and organization, and giving concise reasons and specific solutions to what he saw as the team's problems. When he wrote BALLS, his diary of the 1983 season, a year of chaos and disintegration, Graig Nettles intended to remain a New York Yankee. BALLS was to be a springboard for change, and he was going to be a beneficiary of that change—as a Yankee. This book was called BALLS because it took a person of incredible courage to do what he was doing.

The book was scheduled for publication in the spring of 1984, but first it was to be excerpted in the *New York*

Daily News. The plan was that BALLS was to remain a secret to all until publication. However, someone on the *News* leaked the contents to the Yankee owner, George Steinbrenner, who immediately began spreading stories in the papers that his captain, Graig Nettles, was complaining about having to platoon in 1984 and that he was a negative influence on the other players. Steinbrenner, moreover, told reporters that he had heard that Nettles had been critical of his teammates in his new book, and as a result, said Steinbrenner, Graig Nettles had become a detrimental influence on the team and would have to go. He didn't say that Nettles had been critical of him, mind you, only that he had been critical of his teammates.

Instead of heeding the message in BALLS and considering what Graig Nettles was telling him, George Steinbrenner instead forced Graig Nettles to leave the Yankees. Graig, a veteran, could not be traded without his permission. The only team Graig would agree to go to was San Diego, his hometown. He really didn't want to leave the Yankees, but he knew he had no choice. He had seen the Yankee owner mount whispering campaigns against too many other players while they were still Yankees; teammates like Reggie Jackson, Tommy John and Davey Collins. His manager, Billy Martin, had been fired and exiled. His closest friend, Goose Gossage, absolutely refused to play another year under Steinbrenner, and he had signed with San Diego. Graig knew he had to leave, and that if he didn't leave, the Yankee owner would crucify him in the papers. He was a ballplayer, not a martyr.

The fallout made baseball history. Graig Nettles

played third base for the San Diego Padres and helped lead his new team into the World Series. Without him, his old team, the Yankees, fell into last place early in the season, recovering only when the team began following the advice Graig had laid out in BALLS: stop trying to fill the roster with over-priced stars from other teams and stabilize the team by bringing up the young kids from the minors.

In gratitude, the Yankees at Old-Timers' Day retired his number, 9, honoring Roger Maris but not mentioning Graig. Though Graig couldn't make the ceremony (he wasn't invited), all true Yankee fans were thinking of him, as he continued his brilliant play, three thousand miles away on the other coast.

Graig Nettles will always be remembered for his calm professionalism, for his Hall of Fame performance over the years, and for having the guts to stand up and be heard. Long after his playing career is over, baseball fans will remember Graig Nettles for his diving stops at third, his clutch hitting, and for BALLS.

Harold Robbins

The World's Best Storyteller

When you enter the world of Harold Robbins, you enter a world of passion and struggle, of poverty and power, of wealth and glamour . . .

A world that spans the six continents and the inner secrets, desires and fantasies of the human mind and heart.

Every Harold Robbins bestseller is available to you from Pocket Books.